the Soldier

the Sailor &

the Singer

the Soldier the Sailor & the Singer

Donald O. Burling
and
Dodie Frost

Freesong Publishing

Cover design: OspreyDesign

Book design and production by Tabby House

Publisher's Cataloging-in-Publication
(Provided by Quality Books, Inc.)

Burling, Donald O.
   The soldier, the sailor & the singer / Donald O.
Burling and Dodie Frost. -- 1st ed.
   p. cm.
   Includes index.
   LCCN 00-135662
   ISBN 0-9704581-0-X

   1. Burling, Donald O. 2. Frost, Dodie. 3. Composers
--United States--Biography. 4. Gospel musicians--United
States--Biography. 5. Country musicians--United States
--Biography. 6. World War, 1939-1945--Biography.
7. Christian Science--United States--History. I. Frost,
Dodie. II. Title.

ML390.B87 2001   780'92'2
                          QB100-901954

Freesong Publishing
P.O. Box 1320
Venice, FL 34284
E-mail: freesongbooks@aol.com

In memory and dedication
Captain Jennie Calhoon Burling
The stone on her resting place reads:
We fought the fight, ran the race, and finished last.

If Jennie finished last it was because she was with someone who needed help. Her prize was not at the top of the mountain but in the lives of those who were trying to make the climb.

—Rev. Douglas Passage

My final salute to my greatest friend lies in these pages for a victory of her working and living for God and humanity with all her heart, soul and energy. She was one brave soldier.

—Commander Donald O. Burling, USNR (Ret.)

Contents

Preface

Through the years Donald Oscar Burling made many friends through his world travels, his good deeds and his music. He never intended to write a book about his life, it simply began to happen through his doing and mine. Even though we have never met, we share a most unusual friendship. You could say that we've been pen pals since 1982 when he was instrumental in sending me to Nashville, Tennessee, to record an album for him and his wife, Jennie Calhoon Burling.

In 1981 the Burlings had produced and published an album of music set to Donald's poems and were planning a second when I was contacted. Donald had finished writing ten new poems for Jennie to be set to music. The album was the fulfillment of our shared dream: his to publish his hymns of praise to God and to educate and help people find a better life through his words; mine to uplift and inspire thought with my singing to promote healing.

As I got to know the man behind the beautiful spiritual poems and his beloved wife, I was amazed at the life they had led and continued to lead in their golden years. This book is much more than about a trip to the recording studio and its wonderful aftermath. It is the true story of a man and a woman (a sailor and a soldier) who met on a troopship bound for Bombay during World War II, and about how they lived, worked and loved their God, their country and all of God's children. They shared a remarkable, devoted life together.

Both Jennie and Donald were scholars who researched a wide range of topics. Jennie wrote and talked about her experiences as a female nurse in prewar Iran. She read the Bible eleven times in her later years and was a stalwart leader in her church's Sunday school.

She is remembered by the Rev. Nancy Cook, pastor of the Elbridge Community Church, in Elbridge, New York. Nancy shared with me in a letter that they became very good friends when Jennie was the superintendent of the Sunday school in First Baptist Church Penn Yan. Nancy had been called in to be the interim pastor part time. She wrote of the time when Don had some major surgery in 1987 with some life-threatening complications. She drove to the hospital to be with Jennie while Don was recovering and to be a support for both of them. I could understand through correspondence how her unselfish love must have been felt through their prayers. Nancy reverently recalled how Don had challenged her to preach from the Old Testament because he had never heard anyone from First Baptist preach on an Old Testament text. She said she took the challenge and preached on Isaiah 45: 1-7 using Matthew 27: 15-23 as a side reference. The sermon was titled "God's mysterious grace." From that time on she preached using an Old Testament text with the New Testament. She said she cherishes Don's wisdom for it was a very special learning gift.

The Rev. Douglas Passage, a longtime friend of the Burlings, has sent me numerous letters expressing his interest in and of endearment for them. In his many stories about Jennie's education, service and dedication to her church, friends and strangers, I could see a devotion of mutual ministering. His sermons and his personal accounts were wonderful and so honest and humble. I particularly loved reading his "Wedding Vow Renewal Service" for Don and Jennie, the "Service of Internment for Jennie Burling" and his sermon of "Reflections and Prayer" for his congregation. His words were strengthening to me and satisfied my hunger for knowing more and more about the lives of those around Jennie and Donald and what their love of church and friendships were about.

Donald, a Naval commander, had a distinguished career at sea and used his keen mind to acquire several academic degrees, and to write essays, sermons, pamphlets, prayers, books and the poetry—much of which was put to music for country gospel. I know the impact of his words from having recorded them.

Together they were a couple who helped all in need who came their way. I was impressed to hear of the help they gave to Eliza Moore, an African American woman who met Jennie through the church. Her grandson was in Jennie's Sunday school class. Jennie went to Eliza's home and asked if she could make him mind and sit down when she asked him to. Jennie told Eliza when she had him write numbers he was having problems. She asked Eliza if she could help him with his math. Eliza in turn asked Jennie if she would help *her* with her reading. Jennie said yes, and tutored her for a long time. She was helping her grandson and helping her also. They became good friends.

That is when Eliza told Jennie that she was the last of twelve children in a family in Virginia and when she grew to school age, her mother would not let her go to school. Eliza's mother told her she would never be able to do anything except keep house. So that is what she did. Eliza had in earlier years, migrated north and was married. Her husband was still in Virginia but was not supporting her. Jennie helped her get a divorce and be free from that burden. Eliza was a member of First Baptist Church and was working for the local hospital in housekeeping. Her wages were very low so was not able to improve the structural condition of her house. She was discouraged because repairs were estimated at least $2,500. Jennie talked it over with her. The Burlings had some money left over from the sale of their house in Massachusetts. So they loaned Eliza the money with no interest. She paid it all back within four years. Jennie's compassion helped Eliza become independent.

Eliza would stop in after work every day at the Burlings for her tutoring session. She was a good student because she wanted to learn. Eliza had her eyes set on a promotion to housekeeper for the operating room and surgical area at the hospital. It was a better job with higher pay. Eliza often told the Burlings that she did not think she would ever get anything like that because she was colored and she was in her mid-fifties. But the Burlings helped her gain her self-respect and self-confidence. In spite of the support Eliza had her doubts, but she did succeed and earned the job. Her happiness was spilling over when she stopped by the Burling's house to tell them about it. She finally conceded that the best woman got the job, regardless of color. She continued to get pay increases. She bought a car, a bright red one. She took a driver's education course and got her license. The Burlings shared this story with me and said it was one of the happiest of life experiences they could remember when helping others. They frequently wrote me about what pleasure it gave them to help others.

Eliza sent me a very dear note also sharing the experience with me. She also related a glimpse into the Burling's household. She wrote:

"When I would go to their house for my lessons, Mr. Burling would be getting the dinner, she would always laugh and say, 'I don't know what we are having for dinner, but whatever Donald prepares is what we will have.' Then, Mrs. Burling would do the dishes. Mr. and Mrs. Burling were very devoted to each other. I worried about him when she passed away because I didn't know if he could go on without her, they were so close. There are so many things about the Burlings that I just can't explain. They were just wonderful people. They will always be a part of my life. I can't explain the love I have for those two people."

* * *

As our letters accumulated through the years, I began to realize that we had many shared interests, and that this couple had given much to me through their friendship. They have given me insights of their honesty and wisdom, teaching that if one lives up to his truest sense of worth and self-respect, he can best serve others. I believe Donald and Jennie have proven this in their lives.

Each of us should validate our lives in such a way. I thank them both for their unselfish gift and the opportunity to know them as dearest friends. And I am forever grateful for that call to come to Nashville and record his music.

My life has changed because of the Burlings. To know The Soldier and The Sailor you also need to know The Singer.

DODIE FROST

Part I

The Singer

By Dodie Frost

A New Day

It was a cold dismal morning in February as I drove north into Boston to work. I hadn't worked an eight-to-four job since 1967 when I had left my job shortly before my second child was born. Now it was 1982. Two of my children were in school and one was in the U.S. Air Force and I was having mixed emotions about returning to the same place of employment I had left fifteen years earlier.

As I pulled into the underground garage, I smiled at the security person who greeted me and thought, *How nice to see a smiling face so early in the morning. How nice to have a sheltered garage in which to park this old Chevy station wagon.* The day was starting as so many had back in the 1960s—there was nothing to indicate the change that was about to occur in my life.

Walking into the great open entryway of the building that housed the *Christian Science Monitor*, an international daily newspaper, I looked up at all the flags hanging overhead representing the countries of the free world. The elevator door opened and I pushed the button to the fifth floor. I recalled that the building had been constructed in 1929. The wood finish in the elevator was very warm and appealing to the eye. I had grown to love and appreciate the building that had been my home away from home and remembered riding this elevator to the sixth floor in 1965 when I was working for the editors of the periodicals. Now I would be working for the associate editors on the floor below, down the hall from the translations department.

The phone was ringing as I stepped into my office, and I picked up the receiver. "Hello, this is Doreen Taylor," I announced. The person on the other end asked for Dodie Frost, which is the stage name I only used away from the office. "Speaking," I replied, "May I ask who's calling?" The man explained in a very southern accent, "Why, this is Roy Callaway in Nashville." Suddenly, I remembered being told by Ted Rosen of Talent Inc., a recording studio where I worked part time, that one of his songwriters wanted me to go to Nashville to make a record. Roy Callaway went on to explain that Donald Burling had asked him to call and set up a recording session in Nashville at the Smokehouse Studios in April.

Donald Burling's name was familiar to me. He had written poems and sent them to the recording studio to be set to music. Through the years I had been recording there, I had arranged and sung several of Donald Burling's lyrics. The words were very devout and showed a marvelous variety of expressions. I thanked Mr. Callaway and assured him I would see him in April, leaving until later the details of taking time off from my new job and making arrangements for someone to stay with my children.

So many thoughts ran through my mind during the rest of that day. It was not happenstance that brought my voice and Donald Burling's lyrics together. He was familiar with my singing from the demo records that we cut in the recording studio. I had often been handed his lyrics, had composed a melody to go with them and then a copy was sent to him in Penn Yan, New York. It was starting to become obvious that we had been preparing for something bigger than we anticipated.

Donald had no way of knowing what I experienced when I was fifteen years old. He wouldn't know until years later, as our friendship developed. But I had a stirring in my thoughts that reminded me of this youthful experience.

I loved playing records—both the 78 rpm and 331/3s. My parents had a record collection of big band music, classical, religious and opera (recordings of the Great Caruso). There was one album that my mother put on for me to listen to when I was fifteen and suffering from an inflamed skin condition. My appearance was alarming. The album collection was that of hymns with a tenor singing, accompanied by an organ. One caught my attention—the hymn "Christ My Refuge," with words written by Mary Baker Eddy. As I grasped the spiritual significance of its message, my appearance changed. My skin softened and the ugliness dissolved. The experience changed my disposition as well as the direction of my life. I wrote a letter to the tenor, Mr. Jagel, after finding his address on the back of the album. I told him of my experience and he wrote back on blue stationery, thanking me and inviting me to study with him in Boston after I graduated from high school. We corresponded and two years later, in May 1959, my parents drove me to Massachusetts. I became a resident of the Benevolent Association in Chestnut Hill. I found my way by trolley to Huntington Avenue in Boston to the New England Conservatory of Music where I studied with Frederick Jagel. It was a time to grow musically and vocally.

Another experience came to mind while I was preparing for my trip to Nashville, that made me realize this was a mission of promise, one that I would share some day with Donald Burling.

In 1965 my husband and I were in New York City attending an association and decided to visit a branch church we had not visited before—the Fifth Church of Christ, Scientist. Before the Bible lesson was read from the desk, a tenor sang a solo that I was very familiar with. It wasn't just another service or just another soloist. An usher told me the tenor's name was George Sawtelle. I had never heard of him, but his voice was full of warmth and clarity and his words interpreted with meaning and excellence. I had no way of knowing that someday I would meet

George Sawtelle in the Christian Science Publishing House broadcast building and that we would be selected to record an album together in New York City in 1973. The album, "His song shall be with me," were hymns set to orchestral accompaniment. It was something I could never have envisioned nor planned.

In 1968 I found a position (from an ad in the *Boston Globe*) as a song stylist for a recording studio outside Boston, that gave me a fine opportunity to record music of all kinds of styles and rhythms.

Other thoughts ran through my mind while preparing for the trip to Tennessee. I considered how many times I had seen Donald's name on the lyrics he sent in for review. The studio's owner and staff would have the work all laid out for me. There were numerous lyrics and corresponding letters flowing into the very busy single-owner recording company. I never knew where all the song writers were from except when a few special letters were pointed out to me and shared. The staff handled all that. My input in composition and interpretation was my job and I spent long hours in the recording studio singing those compositions. I wanted to satisfy and please the lyric writers—to give them voice for their words. I remember especially that Donald's words always had a direction. If the path were dark the words would lead you to the light. If sad, he would show you how to find joy. His songs gave solutions. That was what I worked for in my singing—to stir the troubled thought to a healthy thought.

My desire was to sing with inspiration, to uplift thought and to encourage healing. I wanted the songs to make a difference for the listener. I didn't want to just sing it like it was just another song, but a song that would live forever. That is what Donald wanted, too. That is what I had experienced from the voice of Frederick Jagel and the words of Mary Baker Eddy. That is what I would share with many willing audiences and listeners hungry for inspiration. And it would happen with Donald's words. I just knew it.

I learned that the words for the ten songs for Donald and his wife, Jennie's, new album were already in the hands of the composer-arranger in Nashville. Everything was being provided for me. Donald sent me a check for plane fare and asked that I keep track of my expenses so he could take care them. I hadn't been at my job long enough to have earned vacation time, but my employers kindly told me to take the time I needed.

* * *

It was April all right. The tulips were in full bloom. I had forgotten how beautiful spring is in the South. The photographs for the cover of the album were taken in the gardens in the center of Nashville near the famous Parthenon, just a few blocks away from Country Row. Around the corner were the big studios and offices of Capitol Records, RCA and Columbia. I had been picked up from the airport and driven to my hotel by way of the recording sites. We pulled into a driveway and there, nestled in between two other private studios, was a white stucco house with a garden entry leading to the doorway. It was Smokehouse Studios, where I would spend the next five days recording. We went in. It was a beautiful sight—like none I had seen before. The studio in Quincy was efficient and small quartered. The one in New York where I recorded in 1973 was enormous—large enough to house an orchestra, with soundproof rooms for the soloists. But this was something else. Donald had chosen the Benson Company (Great Circle Records) to record his songs because it was the best Christian recording company in Nashville. The studio staff welcomed me to Nashville. It was well designed, cozy and with high-tech equipment. Every corner was utilized. I was told that BJ Thomas and Eddie Arnold had also recorded there, and that the engineer I'd be working with was Elvis Presley's soundman for eleven years near the end of his career.

I was told they had the utmost respect for Donald Burling and his dear wife, then in their late seventies. They said they would do all in their power to produce a quality album. And they certainly did.

Music came early

The name on my birth certificate is Doreen Berry Frost. I was born a twin into a family with religious and moral values and parents with a great love for music, travel and a zest for life. My mother, Beverly Bond (Wilson) Frost, was born in Framingham, Massachusetts, on March 25, 1921, and later moved to New Jersey. My father, Frederic Vincent Frost, was born in Lyndhurst, New Jersey, on December 26, 1918. My parents met in Atlantic City, New Jersey, in the summer of 1939. They were both working musicians during that summer and met on the beach.

My father enjoyed performing. He sang and played string bass fiddle in dance bands in New York and New Jersey with many great artists of the time. He worked with the Dorsey Brothers, Glenn Miller and Nat "King" Cole. He loved telling how he met Cole when he was a young man just starting out in New York City. My mother played violin in a string quartet, entertaining in the big hotels. She started playing violin at an early age. In her high school year, she held the position of first chair of the first violin section for the All State Orchestra of New Jersey. She was an accomplished violinist.

My mother and father fell in love and eloped. My father enlisted in the Army, shortly after World War II began. My parents were living in East Orange, New Jersey, when my twin and I were born at the Essex County Hospital on the 29th of December 1941 (the same month of the surprise attack on Pearl Harbor). It was a challenging time for the country and of course for my parents. I followed my twin sister, Diana Bond Frost, into a troubled world at a very troubled time in history.

That was the time when food was rationed and victory gardens were planted. Our father even raised chickens and tried to maintain some stability to our lives. We were three years old when our father was stationed in Jacksonville, Florida.

Our little brother, Douglas Frederic Frost, was born on November 11, 1946, in the Army Hospital in Jacksonville, Florida. It was Armistice Day.

Transfer papers came through from the Army for our family to move to Memphis, Tennessee. I was too young to understand what my parents were experiencing. We were being moved again and my father was sent from Memphis to Tokyo in June 1950. It was the beginning of the Korean War. We didn't know if we would ever see him again.

No military families were allowed to travel to Japan for a very long time. It was eighteen months before we finally got word we could join my father overseas. I loved and missed him terribly. I wrote a paper in English about it when I was thirteen years old. Got an "A interesting/A-" from my English teacher. My story reads as follows:

The night I told daddy good-bye

One cool morning in October, I was awakened by the motor of my father's car. I sat up in bed and opened the blinds to watch him as he drove off to work. I knew I would see him at supper. However, there was a time when I hadn't seen him for eighteen months.

Daddy joined the armed forces when I was very young, causing us to be transferred from Jersey, to Florida, then to Tennessee.

On my seventh Christmas, Daddy gave my twin sister and me a big twenty-six-inch bicycle. He spent a great deal of time with us, teaching us how to ride and care for it. Oh, I loved to be with him so much.

The very next April, which I remember so well, Daddy came home in his uniform. I gazed at him like a child would at a bright light. Then he had to destroy this wonder by telling us he was leaving home to live in a foreign country.

I went upstairs to bed that evening wondering if he loved us anymore. Otherwise, why would he want to leave us? I climbed into bed with a heavy heart and cried myself to sleep.

9

It seemed only a short time later, when my bedroom door opened. I lay very still as a strong warm hand lightly smoothed my blond hair from my cheek. A deep but tender voice whispered softly in my ear, "Take care of Mommy for me while I'm away, and it won't be long until we will be together again." I answered in a whisper as I closed my eyes very tightly to keep the tears back, "I promise, Daddy—good-bye."

* * *

The summer of 1951 came and my mother decided it would be good for my sister and me to stay with Grandma and Grandpa Frost in New Jersey while she worked. My sister and I had a great summer with our grandparents. We got to hear all kinds of stories about how my grandmother, Maple Berry (Frost) and her sister Dorothy Berry left New Jersey when they were three and five years old and traveled West to settle in Taylor, North Dakota. They were cowgirls who rode horseback on the prairies.

There were all kinds of pictures and remnants from the West in the Frost household. My sister and I can still describe the house and its contents. There was so much love in my grandparents' home. There were so many rooms in their house; they rented out a couple of rooms like a boarding house. My grandmother belonged to the Methodist Church and gave me a Bible, which I still have and cherish to this day. The summer passed quickly.

While my father was in Japan I used to listen to the radio at night to hear news broadcasts and country music. As I listened to the music, I'd think how close Nashville was and all the famous country singers. I would remember how my father would sing to me. He would imitate Hank Williams and Gene Autry and even attempt yodeling, something I could never do in spite of all the vocal antics I'd attempt. I had a great love for Gene Autry, a singing cowboy who wrote his own songs and did his own stunts on horseback in the movies. When Gene Autry was touring Tennessee, my mother took, me to see him perform in person. In my eyes, Gene Autry was a substitute for my missing daddy.

On the troopship the USS *Ulysses S. Grant* that transported us over to Yokohama, my sister, brother and I watched movies below deck with the other military children. The Army provided us with all the favorite movies. I was especially happy when they played a Gene Autry movie. We docked in Yokohama on December 7, 1951, the tenth anniversary of Pearl Harbor. There were hundreds of soldiers waiting for their families, just like my mother and father. My mother picked him out of the crowd as he ran to us and embraced us. We all cried together. What a relief it was and a very happy moment. We were then taken to foreign customs, fingerprinted and issued dog tags, given a military identification card and military currency.

We lived in Grant Heights, a military base located thirteen miles outside of Tokyo. That is when I started writing poems, singing in the school glee club and playing piano. Mother and Dad purchased a three-quarter violin for Diana while they shopped in the Ginza area of downtown Tokyo.

When the U.S. Army moved us back to the States, we traveled sixteen days on the ocean during Christmas and New Year's. We were traveling on the USS *James O'Hara*, a troopship en route to Seattle, Washington. My dad was given a Santa Claus suit provided by the Army so he could play the role. He distributed gifts for all the ship's passengers. That included those in the cabins below with soldiers, their war brides and babies.

We survived a typhoon on the high seas as we neared the Aleutian Islands and docked in Adak, Alaska. The Army had to leave Korean War wounded soldiers there to be transported to hospitals. There were a lot of injuries on the ship as well. I was very young, but remember it vividly.

While my dad was a veteran of the United States Army he earned the American Campaign Medal and the World War II Victory Medal in 1945. During the Korean War, he trained soldiers for combat at Camp Drake from 1950 until 1952.

11

After two weeks at Fort Lewis near Seattle, we took a train across country coast to coast. We moved in with my Grandma Frost in Nutley, New Jersey, until my father's new orders came through. I loved being with my grandmother again. I missed my Grandpa. He was very ill while we were in Japan and passed away just before Christmas in 1951.

My dad transferred from the Army Intelligence Office to become a civilian contract agent for the Naval Investigation Service Headquarters in Charlotte, North Carolina. Dad chose Charlotte of all the places to live because he wanted his children to have good schools and a friendly environment. He was right. The schools had very successful music programs. We were also very involved in our church activities. My father moved us one more time and that was to Greensboro, North Carolina, where my sister and I graduated from high school. Diana and I later moved to Boston, Massachusetts, to attend The New England Conservatory of Music.

My father took a very important position in the Office of Naval Intelligence in Washington, D.C. He served under President Kennedy and then for the Johnson administration. My parents lived very modestly in their senior years and their marriage endured fifty-two years. My mother passed away November 25, 1992 on the eve of Thanksgiving. My father passed away on February 4, 1995. He was given a military burial and is buried at San Joaquin Valley in California in the military cemetery.

* * *

The move to Boston from North Carolina in 1959 gave me the opportunity to study with Frederick Jagel at the New England Conservatory of Music. After two years, he encouraged me to study with Chloe Owen at the Boston University School of Fine Arts, also in the field of opera and the classics.

Other opportunities opened up for me while I was in Boston, such as working for a modeling agency and performing with a theater group and in choral groups as well as the occasional solo performances. These put me more in the public spotlight on stage, radio and television. An agent who was a talent scout for supper clubs and country clubs around Boston saw me. We signed contracts and I became a member of the American Guild of Variety Artists. In order for me to perform with house orchestras and artists from New York, Las Vegas and Miami I needed to be in a national musicians union. I met and worked with many famous artists who came to the Monticello and Blinstrub's. I had the opportunity to do the same circuit and to be introduced on the Johnny Carson Show in California, but chose not to travel. I had a family and I decided to work close to home.

When the supper clubs were taken over by the large hotels' function rooms, the music business changed and I had to change with it. The large house orchestras downsized to band combos. So I established my own five- and four-piece bands. As much as I loved the electric bass in my bands I even had to forego that and look for a keyboardist who could play left-handed bass as well as lead. After going through several changes of musicians I found a keyboard player from Bellingham, Massachusetts. He was the root of the band we called Dodie Frost and Company. Later I had a guitarist and a drummer who worked well together until we dissolved in 1999. We were very much in demand and entertained a variety of music from the oldies, through the ages to the current top hits, show tunes and theater. We performed all around New England in restaurants and hotels. The most memorable were the annual military balls in Newport, Rhode Island. The band members gave me their talents and their friendships and enriched my life.

In 1982, my twin sister, Diana, was the chairman of the entertainment committee for the Chamber of Commerce in Peabody, Massachusetts. She told me the city had won the bid for the first women's world softball tournament to be held in the state and it needed a jingle for advertising and a theme song for the Hall of Fame. This is when I wrote the two songs for the United States

13

Slo-pitch Softball Association, headquartered in Petersburg, Virginia. One was called "Something is Happening at Cy Tenney Park" and the other was "Give Me a Slo-pitch." Copies of the songs were sold on souvenir records to support the chamber and to commemorate the event.

Influence of my mother's family

I never knew my grandfather, Frederick M. Wilson (my mother's father). He passed away under the strain of the Great Depression of 1929. I know that he served in WWI, but I don't know anymore than that. My grandmother, Jessie Davis Wilson, was born and raised in Boscawen (near Bow), New Hampshire, was widowed at the age of forty-five and left as sole supporter of their four children: Barbara Wilson, the oldest daughter, Rosamond Wilson, my mother Beverly and her twin brother, Richard.

My grandmother was a Christian Scientist. She learned how to pray through her study of a book given to her by a close friend. Her friend, who we came to know as Auntie Stephens, was the midwife in attendance at the birth of my mother and her twin brother. The book was the Christian Science textbook entitled *Science and Health with key to the scriptures* by Mary Baker Eddy.

I was told there was a remarkable healing that took place during my grandmother's recovery after the birth of her twins. The twins were skeletal and one was deformed, the other, seemingly lifeless. Grandmother was anemic. At the urging of my aunt and grandmother, the doctor tied the cords of both babies and attended to them at the home delivery. Through the next several months, great love and devotion to prayer brought about their complete recovery, including grandmother's anemia. It marked the beginning of four generations of Christian Scientists in my family. I will always remember her for her dedication to her books. She would read her Bible and the textbook along with her *Christian Science Quarterly*, a daily lesson study, and other writings by Mary Baker Eddy (who lived in Bow, New Hampshire). The books were her

lifelong companion, since she never married again. She demon-
strated longevity. Her last residence was at the Christian Science
Benevolent Association in Chestnut Hill, Massachusetts.

My mother took a two-week course of class instruction of Christian Science in Memphis, Tennessee, in 1950 during the Korean
War while my father was in Japan. She later became a Christian
Science Journal-listed practitioner. It was in Memphis that I remember having a close friendship with our black servant. Because
healing is such a favorable study in my church, I always searched
it out. I had a toy piano and would pick out hymns from my hymnal and sing them and feel joy. I remember playing on a pile of
lumber near my home. I fell and skinned my leg badly. I ran into
the house crying, and in pain. Diana hugged me to comfort me.
Mary (our servant) took out my toy piano and opened my hymnal
to page 88 and started singing "Gracious spirit dwell with me. I
myself would gracious be. And with words that help and heal, would
Thy life in mine reveal. And with actions bold and meek, Christ's
own gracious spirit speak." I was so full of love for her for helping
me that I realized when I went to wash, that the alarm of the acci-
dent had left my mind. I felt comforted and renewed. The scrape
became insignificant. I learned what peace can be felt from singing
about God and our relationship to Him.

During the many moves our family experienced, my mother
searched out the Christian Science churches so that my twin sister,
brother and I were in attendance at the Sunday Schools. Interest-
ingly, while we were in Japan our church services were held in a
nearby building next to the Diet (government) Building in downtown Tokyo. My mother had a book called *The Story of Christian
Science Wartime Activities 1939-1946* that I studied. There were
several pages about the first two Americans to set foot in Tokyo
after Japan's surrender and the activities of Christian Science before the war. I cherished the book and quote: "One was a Staff
Correspondent of the Christian Science Monitor. First among Chris-

tian Science Camp Welfare representatives to arrive were volunteer Wartime Workers, followed later by two chaplains." (Page 317). It is still fascinating reading.

My Sunday school teacher was Mrs. Matsukata (her husband was once premier of Japan). Another member of the church, Mrs. Takaki, took my family on a tour of the emperor's palace grounds. She told me that she was a lady-in-waiting to the empress and tutored her in English with the aid of the *Christian Science Monitor.*

I saw the emperor and empress at the emperor's horse show when my sister and I attended it with our Girl Scout troop. Incidentally, the Christian Science church was constructed and dedicated that year and we were able to be a part of its establishment. I remember the commotion of service men and women greeting a Christian Science teacher and lecturer from Boston named Ralph Wagers.

I didn't know then that I would see him again in my adult years of service in Boston at The Mother Church. And incredibly, his voice is on many recordings of lectures and articles from the periodicals. I also didn't know until my adult years in Boston that I would see another friend whom I had met in Tokyo in 1951. She was Emi Abiko, Japanese translator for the periodicals and working on the fifth floor of the publishing house when I worked there in 1982.

My mother was a pioneer for good and I am forever grateful for her dedication.

Influence of my father's family

My grandmother (my father's mother, Maple Berry) was born October 1881, and her sister, Dorothy, was born March 7, 1879, in New Jersey. In my teenage years it meant a great deal to me to know that my Aunt Dorothy had written and published a book about the Berry Family titled *White Gumbo.* I never knew my great-grandfather, Abraham Bloomfield Berry, but there are pictures of my twin and me with our great-grandmother Annie Berry. My great-grandparents were religious and wanted to raise their daughters in the great open spaces out west. Imagine the way life was then only a few years after Custer's last stand. Abraham Berry (known affectionately as Abie) was a minister and owned the hotel in Taylor, North Dakota. He also had a large sheep ranch named the A-BAR-B Ranch. He raised horses for the government as well as acres of evergreen trees. He was a strong provider for his family. He traded furs with the Indians and was very supportive of Theodore Roosevelt, a trailblazer and a president who, as lieutenant colonel of the First Volunteer Cavalry (the Rough Riders), became a dynamic leader for the nation in 1898. I used my aunt's book for a book report in my junior high school days. I was strongly influenced by grandmother and her family.

They lived there in Taylor until my Aunt Dorothy left the ranch for Fargo to Agricultural College and my grandmother moved back to New Jersey. My grandmother, Maple, married William J. Frost and settled in Nutley, New Jersey. My Aunt Dorothy was a journalist for a newspaper and met Count Julius de St. Clement, an Italian shipping merchant at a formal social. They fell in love. Through correspondence they decided to marry. They were going to marry on the *Titanic,* but Julius couldn't leave Rome because of business. Aunt Dorothy sailed out of New York to Italy. They married January 1913 and resided in his palace, where they lived in grand style. They never had children. After Julius passed away, Dorothy moved back to New Jersey and lived with her sister in Nutley and continued in her journalism. Her book *White Gumbo* was copyrighted in 1951 and dedicated to The Women's Club of Nutley, New Jersey. She also wrote a book of poems entitled *Prairies and Palaces,* published in 1963 and dedicated to: "My beloved husband, Count Giulio de Sauteiron de St. Clement, last scion of his noble family on the borderline of France and Italy." Her poem on the dedication page reads: "Often, when I said I heard / Songs and music in the wind and rain / And everything that stirred, / You tried to hear them, too—and you did, dear heart. / You smiled and voiced approval. / Our love was a thing apart. / This is our poetry." (La Contessa Dorothy de Sauteiron de St. Clement)

My grandmother passed away at eighty-six years of age. Aunt Dorothy died on June 24, 1984. She was one hundred and five years old. I treasure the copy of *White Gumbo* that she autographed for me on her one hundredth birthday and her autographed book of poems.

Part II

The Soldier and the Sailor

By Donald O. Burling

The Soldier and the Sailor

I was born Oscar Donald Bjorling on November 20, 1901, in New London, Connecticut. My father's name was Oscar. He was born and raised in Norrkoping, Sweden, in 1877, the son of the town miller. One day in 1898 he drove a team-load of grain down to the docks near Norrkoping. My father saw a U.S. Coast Guard vessel in the harbor, got a ride to it and enlisted for the war. After the war his ship returned to the United States and was anchored at New Bern, North Carolina. During his stay there, he met and married my mother, Mary Lettis Hart.

She was born in Washington, North Carolina, on the Tar River in 1877, so she was a real Tarheel. Her family came to America in the early colonial days. Mary Queen of Scots had driven out many of the Scots who were not Anglican or Catholic and her family was Presbyterian. They settled in the Vanceboro and Washington, North Carolina, areas.

After my father left the Coast Guard, he went to work for most of his life for the American Bridge Company. He and my mother separated when I was about eight years old . I had a younger brother and sister. We were living in Manhattan during this period. My mother never told me the reason for the split. From then on we were really poor, living on New York's east side near the East River.

We lived in a six-story walk-up tenement building that the city had built for poor people. The rent was about $1.50 a week. We had two bedrooms, a kitchen and a toilet and lavatory. We had no electricity—only gas. The city furnished steam heat.

My mother worked in a cigarette factory about ten blocks away. The city would not let me start school until I was eight years old because of my poor health due to malnutrition and childhood diseases. My mother taught me how to read and write in the meantime. She did it in self-defense. I pestered her so much to read the comics to me, the same ones over and over, that she taught me how to read them myself. When I started school I went through the first three grades in one year.

We attended a Presbyterian mission church on First Avenue, operated by the Fifth Avenue Presbyterian Church. In the middle of my sixth grade the church helped me get accepted by a cooperative school and farm in Maine. It was run by a minister and was supported by this and other wealthy churches and organizations to help poor kids that they considered to be acceptable. It was the Good Will Farm and Schools, on the Kennebec River, about halfway between Waterville and Skowhegan. It ran only seventh grade through twelfth grade.

I left New York in the middle of the sixth grade and was put in the middle of the seventh grade at Good Will. I was a star student in New York, but just barely passed the rest of the seventh grade at Good Will. In the eighth grade I got my old batting average up again (academically speaking) and ended up with a grade of ninety.

Throughout my first two years in high school, I had the second highest average. Only a senior girl beat me out. I can always remember resenting having a girl beat me, but naturally, I know better now; I have learned a lot since.

At the end of my sophomore year my mother pulled me out of school to come home and get a job to help her to support my brother and sister. So I ended my schooling with only five years of elementary and two years of high school, never to receive a high school diploma.

Away from Maine I was not very happy. My English teacher at Good Will had promised to help get me into Dartmouth (his alma mater) at graduation, with a job at the college to help pay my way. Back in New York, my mother was trying to boss me more than I could take. I ran away from home. I gave no notice to my mother, or to my boss in a law office downtown—the job my mother had gotten for me at six dollars a week.

I had very little money. About ten dollars. I headed for the Newsboys' Lodging House in the Bowery. The superintendent took me in. A dormitory bed, bread and milk breakfast was one dollar a week. Next I headed for an employment hall in the Bowery. It was wartime and jobs were available. I got one in a factory, making gaskets for shipboard machinery. The pay was better than the law office, and soon I rented a cubbyhole room at the lodging house for a little bit more. In the meantime my mother found me through the police. They investigated, and between them, the superintendent and my mother, they decided to leave me alone. I was now sixteen. I kept getting raises until I got to eighteen dollars a week. I moved to a nice room in the Morningside Heights area. I saved like a miser. I got to three hundred dollars. I decided to leave town and go west, where I thought the pastures were greener now that the war was over.

I went down to the railroad station and asked the ticket clerk where his trains went. He probably thought I was crazy. I asked him, "How much to Cleveland?" He said, 'Twenty dollars." I said I'd take it. I walked up the street from the station in Cleveland and passed a cheap hotel. I went in, planning to stay a few days while I hunted for a job. But with the war over, the jobs disappeared. I was headed for bankruptcy.

With no other options, I left the hotel for the freight yards. I wasn't sure how I would find a freight car going to Chicago, where I planned to go. I carried only my blanket roll, which held a few clothes. It was nighttime as I wandered among the cars. A watchman stopped me and questioned me. I gave him a story of getting to Chicago and then to Minnesota where I said that I had relatives. He put me on an open coal car and gave me fifty cents. That was big money in 1919. It was March and cold. At Chicago I took the nearest street and just started walking. I had very little money left maybe five dollars. I was in a slum district and passed a cheap-looking building with rooms to rent. I went in. It was a hotel set up for Negroes. I got a room for the night for fifty cents.

* * *

In a strange city, roaming the streets while looking for some kind of work was a desperate and futile project. Nighttime came again. I passed a building that looked like some kind of shelter. I went in and found myself in a Catholic shelter for homeless men. I forget what I told the priest, but I did tell him that I was not Catholic. The priest gave me my first good meal in several days and gave me lodging. The next morning he took me down to the Navy Recruiting Station. I was only seventeen but lied and said I was eighteen, keeping the same birth date. He succeeded in getting the recruiting sergeant to enlist me. I never told the priest that I was under age. I never corrected my birth date until 1936, when Social Security started and I had to get a birth certificate.

The recruiters put me on my way to Great Lakes Naval Training Station. I did not know how to pray, and still God took care of me perfectly, just as if I had done a lot of praying.

At Great Lakes I became a chum with a boy named Darrel Sandifer. He was a direct descendant of George Washington, but I did not know that at the time. He had just graduated from high school down in southern Illinois in the Greenville area. He took me home to his family on leave periods and they took me in like one of their own.

One day Darrel came to me and said that there was a notice on the bulletin board offering one hundred appointments to the Naval Academy from the enlisted ranks. The program had just started the previous year. The men were to be under twenty years old and would be given a preliminary examination in high school work. If we passed this exam we would be sent to a naval preparatory school for preparatory instruction for the actual entrance exam. There were two or three prep schools in different sections of the country. Men who scored in the highest one hundred across the country got the appointments.

Darrel wanted me to sign up with him. I told him that I would not have a chance because I only had two years of high school, but he told me to sign up anyway. I did, and we both passed the preliminary test. We were ordered to the prep school at Newport, Rhode Island. On the rail trip to Boston we had about thirty men. Darrel fell sick on the way and at Newport he was placed in the hospital. He never came back, a victim to the countrywide flu epidemic of 1919–1920. So I lost the boy who was to be my roommate at the Naval Academy. I later got pneumonia but recovered. His mother and father, Susie and Albert Sandifer, took me in as sort of a substitute, and loved and encouraged me for several years.

I passed the entrance exam. Albert was well placed in Republican politics in Illinois. He was not a politician, but was a high school principal. He knew his way around, especially because of his ancestry. He persuaded Senator William McKinley, son of the assassinated president, to give me one of his appointments to the Naval Academy. After the entrance exams Senator McKinley checked and found out that I had passed. As less than one hundred passed I was assured of an enlisted man's appointment. I suggested that Senator McKinley should let me go ahead with my enlisted appointment so that he could use his personal appointment for some other boy. I had a tough time plebe year because of my high school shortfall, but I did pass. I was in the bottom ten percent of the class. I finally caught up during the next three years and ended up with an average for the full four years twelve percent down from the top of my class. Each year was weighted differently, with senior year counting three or four times as much as plebe year. My excellence in mathematics was a key factor.

During the last two years, I stood number seven in my class in navigation. I dearly loved the subject and was determined to conquer it completely. I cannot brag, however, because of the man who ranked number one. He had an average between 3.9 and 4.0, the perfect score, for the two years. I only had a 3.6, but it was considerably behind the class leader.

Nellie Titus, whose mother was a sister of Albert Sandifer, Darrel's father, attended my graduation. After the ceremony, I accompanied Nellie home to Illinois. I tried to get Nellie to marry me, but she was already committed to someone else. She knew that she would not likely marry the man as the relationship was tottering. I was too impatient to wait and later in December of 1925 I married Flora Hord, a school teacher whose family was always close to Nellie's family. Nellie later married and became Nellie Altorn. We still continue our precious contacts every Christmas.

I went to work for Southwestern Bell in St. Louis. My boss was an Army officer and we got along fine. He was eventually transferred to A.T. & T. in New York. In 1933 I was laid off in the third wave of layoffs after the 1929 crash and continuing Depression. Later in the year my former boss called me at my wife's parents' home in Keyesport in Southern Illinois, and offered me a job in Springfield, Massachusetts, where he was then division manager in New England Telephone. I accepted and remained with New England Telephone until my retirement in 1960.

My son, Darrel, was born in 1930 in St. Louis. Freddie was born in 1936 in Springfield, Massachusetts. I became manager at the Westfield office, and later at Lancaster, New Hampshire. While at Lancaster I was called to active duty in October 1940. I had risen to lieutenant senior grade in the active Naval Reserve, and at that time I was commanding officer of the Reserve Division at Springfield.

After five years of marriage, Flora and I became quite estranged. There were never close confidences between us and she withheld much information from me. There was never any problem of sex as she was the very best performer in the bedroom that I have ever had relations with in my whole life. It was in other matters much more important. I will note two strong examples here, but there were many other lesser ones. One Christmas season she was working in a department store in St. Louis as the head of the women's wear department. One evening she called me and asked me to meet her at the trolley near our home. She got off the trolley and said she had been laid off. She never told me why.

Soon after that I visited the department store to find out for myself, and I was shown to a detective. I gave him a story of my being a friend of the family and wanted to help Flora, as by this time I was very suspicious and didn't want him to know that I was her husband. He said that they arrested her for shoplifting. He showed me the items—bras, stockings, etc.—that they found on her when they searched her. She also did some tinkering at the cash register. I thanked him and said I would try to help her.

I never in all my life breathed a word to Flora, nor did I ever pump her for more information. I waited patiently for a genuine confession. It never came. She evidently thought that I was pretty stupid and she just let it stay that way.

Another problem came while we lived in Springfield. When her mother died Flora went to Illinois for the funeral and to help with the after-funeral events. When she returned home she never told me about anything, including about her mother's will. Flora's father was a retired physician, one of the best in that area and a great fellow to know. His greatest avocation passion was farming. He owned a very large amount of the best bottomland soil tracts in that area of the Kaskaskia River. He had seven children—two sons and five daughters. When his widow died it was common knowledge that the estate was willed into seven equal parts. I also had knowledge that one of the sons, a farmer with his own excellent farmland, was trying to buy certain tracts left to the daughters. But Flora never explained anything to me when she returned home.

I never saw one cent of Flora's inheritance and never heard one word of what it was. She was completely silent about that will as long as I lived with her. I kept my peace, never pushing her, and she accepted silence as dumbness. I assumed that she deposited it in her bank out home in Illinois. There were many other instances of more minor withholding of confidences that are usually shared by truly loving partners, but I kept my peace, waiting for the right time to break away. The main thing in that respect was the welfare of my two sons, Darrel and Fred. I was called to active duty and sent to sea. I was on continuous sea duty, separated from Flora physically, for the entire five years of the war.

After closing out my reserve division in Springfield, I was sent to the USS *West Point*, which was being fitted out as a troopship in Norfolk. The crew consisted of the reserve divisions from Springfield, Worcester, Portland, the four Boston divisions and a large number of key Navy personnel. Our job, with three other troopships, was to transport British troops all over the world. On one trip we carried 6,000 Canadian troops from Halifax to Singapore. Pearl Harbor was hit when we were only two days out of Cape Town, where our convoy was to stop for fueling. And Roosevelt and all America condemned Japan for playing such a rotten trick on us. That smelled a bit like hypocrisy. I remember when we landed in Cape Town that Ian Smuts, prime minister, invited our officers to a banquet to celebrate our formal entry into the war. The one phrase that I remember Smuts roaring out with was, "We finally got them into it." And the crowd roared with him.

We unloaded 20,000 troops in Singapore. The British had no more planes and no antiaircraft guns that could reach the Japanese bombers that were bombing us every hour on the hour at high level. We were docked just opposite the power station, which I thought was the most dangerous spot. We never got hit. But the *Wakefield* (the former *Manhattan* of the U.S. lines; we were the former *America*) had her entire bow blown off. She was docked next astern of us.

I found out on a later trip into Bombay why we never got hit. I went up to the British pay office to change some South African money into Indian rupees. I met a young officer that I remembered on our trip to Singapore. He had been wounded and had a nice job in the pay office. He told me that the Japanese commander and the British commander had a gentlemen's agreement that the Japanese would not bomb the power station. They agreed for it to go to the winner intact. Some war! Before leaving Singapore we loaded up with 6,000 refugees.

We got out of Singapore one week before the surrender. Already planning to get a divorce from my wife, early on the trip I made friends with one of the female passengers—my first date on board. She was the wife of General Allenby, the British commander in the Near East. We brought them back to England, but after Pearl Harbor we carried only American troops. Sometimes we brought back refugees. On one return trip we stopped at Casa Blanca and brought back 6,000 Italian prisoners of war. They were not under guard and many did most of the messing duties in feeding them. They were happy to be out of it, were sympathetic with our side, and proved to be very trustworthy.

Our own troops always included two companies of Army nurses. Their quarters were near my stateroom. They were also officers. I decided to make friends with one of them on each trip. My purpose was not mainly for pleasure, although I will confess that it was a very pleasing and rewarding by-product. As I knew that I would never return to Flora, I felt this was a good opportunity to survey for a future wife.

I studied each date on every trip, and kept a notebook with names, home addresses, and some telephone numbers. Only two of the names were not those of nurses. One was a woman that I met in Melbourne and whom I called and dated whenever our ship visited that port, which was several times. Another, Sophie, was a refugee from England. She was Jewish and her family escaped from Holland early in the war and went to England to relatives. She was born in Upstate New York, then her family later returned to Europe. Sophie is the one I chose to settle for at the end of the war.

After two years on the USS *West Point*, I was sent to the USS *President Monroe*, a large troopship, as executive officer. It was in Portland, Oregon, being fitted out for troop service. After a few trips and while anchored in San Francisco, I got hurry-up orders to report to the USS *Cascade*, a destroyer-tender (a large floating Navy yard). She was anchored in Honolulu and was ordered to the South Pacific for the beginning of MacArthur's drive up the Western Pacific. They had twenty officers on board and none of them could navigate. I was specifically ordered as navigator, which was unusual in the Navy. Commanding officers and executive officers are always specific. Other orders are simply "for duty," as determined by the executive officer. The *President Monroe* was also ordered to Honolulu so I got a ride on it there to pick up my next assignment.

I navigated the *Cascade* from Honolulu down to the tiny little island of Funa Futi, almost to Australia. It was our first headquarters on the way to Japan, an eighteen-month drive. At Funa Futi I was assigned duty as a pilot, piloting ships, Navy and otherwise, in and out of harbors. An experienced civilian pilot trained me. He was alone and needed help. I piloted all types of vessels, from the Hornet and the North Carolina down to the lowest Liberty ship.

Partway up the line we got a new captain, Herbert Gates. He was a classmate of mine at the Naval Academy. I soon was made executive officer on the *Cascade* and later got command of my own warship. It was the USS *Vega*, designated as an AK, which is a cargo ship. This ship was special, a sort of engineering ship. We carried a company of Seabees who were engine mechanics. We took all of the cargo landing-craft coming out from the States, and the Seabees installed outboard engines on them. They were used to move cargo from merchant ships anchored in the harbor up onto the sandy beaches on all of the islands that we used for headquarters on the way north. Docking piers for the merchant ships were not possible on those sandy beaches.

I finally made it to Okinawa. One end of the island was still occupied by Japanese troops. Our two battleships would go out at dawn every day and pound them with fourteen-inch shells. Our Marines kept trying to finish them. The battleships would return to anchorage at dusk. It was like commuting to and from work every day. We put up smoke coverage every night. One night our antiaircraft gunner got one of the bombers in his sights through a break in the smoke cover. He let go and brought it down. It fell right onto the main runway on shore that our bombers used every day. They had a tough time getting the runway cleared for the next morning, but the admiral never bawled me out.

I finally got orders to take my ship back to our homeport, San Diego, for repairs. I was almost back to Honolulu when the war ended. I took on fuel at Pearl Harbor and then had a very difficult time trying to get a responsible officer to release my ship so that I could continue to San Diego. They were celebrating at all of the saloons. I finally got away and got to San Diego. It looked like quite a long stay for repairs. So, I contacted Sophie, who was living in Boston, and she decided to come out to San Diego. I rented a room for us so that she would have a place to stay. I soon got orders to leave San Diego and go to Los Angeles and then to San Francisco. The Navy decided not to repair the *Vega*, but decommission it and send it to the ship graveyard in San Francisco. I left Sophie in San Diego until I knew more about our movements.

There was a lot of preliminary work to do while we stayed anchored. I sent for Sophie and rented a Quonset hut apartment on the base. They had a great many of them for naval personnel. There was a commissary store available. I would give myself overnight leave every night, come home to Sophie and return to the ship every morning—a very happy time.

We had to transfer the men, bit by bit as they could be released. I was offered command of another ship or release from active duty. I chose release from active duty and got orders to return to Boston for release. Sophie and I had a nice trip by rail across country to Boston. There I was released from active duty as commander, the rank I achieved during the Pacific drive from Australia up to Okinawa. I was given four months accumulated leave with full pay. I had only a few days leave during my five and one-half years in the war.

I stayed with Sophie's family while waiting assignment from the New England Telephone Company. I was given a job as commercial engineer for the Brockton District. I stayed first at the local hotel, then rented an apartment. Sophie accompanied me for the next two years. Flora remained in Portland, Oregon, with the children and the furniture. I had determined never to return to her, but I had to wait for her to institute divorce proceedings.

In 1947 Flora returned East on her own. I had bought a three-family house with one apartment vacant in anticipation of her return. When she arrived in Brockton, I took her to the apartment and left her to organize the furniture and get settled. I think she was shocked when she discovered that I was not staying with her. But instead I returned to Sophie in our apartment.

I visited Flora from time to time, even eating supper with her and the children. I supported her the best that I could. When she finally realized that I would never live with her again, she contacted a lawyer and started divorce proceedings. The divorce was granted on October 6, 1947. The alimony took nearly half of my pay. The divorce became final April 7,1948. I was finally free to live a normal life.

While living with Sophie, she broke off the relationship twice. There was never any problem between us really, but her family was the problem. We still wanted each other very much. Her family, mainly her mother, liked me very much. But they did not want us to marry. Instead, they wanted Sophie to marry a Jewish man. She gave in to their pressures to end the relationship twice, but came back to me. The third time that she broke off, I felt that I could not continue that way. I studied all of the entries in my notebook that I kept on the *West Point*. I remembered Jennie, contacted her and went to Penn Yan by rail (I had no car) a few times to meet her family and discuss plans. First I proposed that we live together without marriage. She would have no part of that.

Jennie had a relationship with another man for eight years before the war, but did not live with him. They were going to marry but the war came along. Her partner joined the Army as an enlisted man, while she became an officer. Jennie would not ignore regulations regarding fraternizing between enlisted personnel and officers. He would not take that and they broke off. She was not a virgin and knew the score all too well. I considered that she was well worth keeping and I proposed marriage. She wanted time to consider it. In the meantime Sophie called me and wanted to come back. I told her that I had a commitment to Jennie and would only take her back if Jennie turned down my proposal. I agreed to continue the relationship with Sophie without living together and only until I got an answer from Jennie. Jennie proved to be a very smart woman. She accepted me. That ended my relationship with Sophie.

Through it all, though, Sophie was a tremendous blessing for me. She supported me and served me well from the time that I met her on the USS *West Point* until the time that Jennie accepted me. We had corresponded through the rest of the war.

In the end, God rewarded Sophie very well. She was not a young chicken. We were both forty-six when we broke off. God gave her a well-to-do Jewish husband. He had been appointed a top aide to the mayor of Boston because he controlled and held the Jewish vote for the mayor's party in Chelsea, a Jewish city.

Sophie and I continued to exchange greetings during the holidays. I would send her a Hanukkah card and she would send me a Christmas card. Recognizing our past relationship, Jennie gave me her letters unopened. Sophie's husband died a few years ago and left her well off. She died recently at the age of ninety.

God sent her to me to help me through the greatest crisis of my life—the reality of estrangement. Her husband gave her far more than I could ever have given her. God saved Sophie, Jennie and me in a very interesting and somewhat complicated human drama. Flora finally got a job at the Brockton Public Library, from which she retired many years later. She died in Brockton in 1984. Darrel and Freddie took care of her. Darrel stuck with me all the way but Flora succeeded in causing Freddie to hate me to this day. However, Freddie's wife stuck by us and she brought their children up to Braintree to see Jennie and me before we left for Penn Yan.

* * *

Jennie was born in Middlesex, New York, on December 23,1909. We married May 8, 1948, at her brother's home in Elmira. When she arrived in Massachusetts with me, we lived in my apartment in Dorchester. Soon we moved to an apartment in Holbrook, which was close to my job in Brockton, and in 1950 we built a home in Braintree. Jennie changed jobs after two years at a hospital in Weymouth. A comrade nurse worked in the Braintree High School as head of the home economics department and persuaded the principal to hire Jennie for the position of high school nurse. During an eight-year period Jennie attended night school, mostly at Boston University, and earned her bachelor's degree in education. No nursing school taught any courses that would help her in her high school job. She graduated in 1964. Jennie held that job for seventeen years until she retired in 1971. That is when we moved to Penn Yan.

During the years up to 1960, I held two other jobs as manager in Lynn and then in Boston. I retired in 1960 after thirty-three years credit with the Bell system. While still with the company, I attended night school at Bridgewater State College and earned my master's degree in education in 1960. I obtained my teaching certification in a number of classifications, including high school math, elementary teacher and principal, school psychologist, and school guidance counselor and director. I taught for five years in Middleboro and Silver Lake, Massachusetts. Then I retired for good.

During my duty on the USS *Cascade,* a destroyer tender, I wrote a book on the life of Jesus titled *Beloved Jew.* I was an avid Biblical scholar. I did the best I could with the scanty information available at that time. It was published in Boston in 1947. When I retired from teaching in 1967, I tackled writing a book titled *From Tekoa to Tarsus* on the major prophets including the Maccabees, Jesus and Paul. I was teaching a seventh-grade class on the prophets in our Sunday school at All Souls Church in Braintree, which we attended. I did spend a very great deal of time at the Braintree Public Library, studying all the books in their religion section that pertained to the prophets and Jesus. Even without the availability of the Dead Sea Scrolls, I learned a lot. I learned that Jesus's birth date was in 7 BC from astronomers who traced the conjunction of Jupiter and Saturn, forming the brightest star ever, back to 7 BC. I learned that Jesus did survive the cross, one way or another, take your pick. I learned that he continued missionary work, but definitely not in Judea or Israel. I knew that it was in a foreign land but there were no specifics. I felt it might be in South America, traveling in a Phoenician merchant ship, since they were sailing all over the world at that time. When the Dead Sea Scrolls were finally discovered, we knew that the foreign country was the Roman-Greek Empire, right next door. My book had a lot of technical errors in it, but was much closer to the truth than much of the Biblical stories handed down to us by Emperor Constantine in the early fourth century, when he revised fifty percent of the New Testament including ninety percent of the Book of John. My book on the prophets was also a failure.

I then turned to writing hymns that would be acceptable to most faiths. I wrote nearly one hundred, hiring songwriters to put most of them to music. I produced two albums of ten hymns each. The Benson Company in Nashville produced the first album with singers on their staff. Mustard Seed Records in Nashville produced the second with a singer of my choice, Dodie Frost.

Dodie did a lot of her employment at a recording studio in Quincy, Massachusetts. She was an excellent singer and also an excellent composer. When I learned that she composed the music for, and sang, all or most of my hymns, I persuaded her to go to Nashville and record an album for me containing ten of my hymns. The album displays her full picture and the title "Dodie Frost" on the front of the cover. Dodie eventually put together her own little band and performed concerts, especially around her home in the Attleboro, Massachusetts, area.

Her band mostly played variety music, but also included some Christian country music. She gives our hymns full exposure whenever she can. I say "our hymns" because I have given her full copyright and ownership of the songs on the album. We have always been faithful friends and have helped each other in areas where we both needed help.

* * *

When Jennie and I moved to Penn Yan, our first job was to put our home in good modern condition. Our home in Braintree was paid for and we used most of the funds from its sale to renovate the Penn Yan home. We were busy on this project for five or six years doing a lot of the work ourselves, renovating the plumbing and electric, painting, wallpapering and tiling, and hired workers to do the big stuff, such as creating modern cabinets.

After settling in, we then went to work at the First Baptist Church—where Jennie had attended church as a child. The Sunday school had gone down hill; there were only eight young children left. The large all-purpose room on the second floor was divided into rooms with the hard curtains running on overhead tracks. The nursery was in a large room downstairs. The minister had an 11- by 10-foot cubicle upstairs at the end of the all-purpose room. The secretary had a small office forty feet away, across the whole length of the large space. The entire layout was not practical. The minister was one of the finest in the business. He got together with Jennie to discuss remedies. They decided on a grand scheme of reallocating the available space. The minister sold the plan to the trustees, as it would cost several thousands of dollars to tear down walls, and additional electric lines, add two toilets, install cabinets in the new Sunday school layout, and overall mammoth rearranging of the Sunday school space.

The large space on the first floor was made into what we called a Fellowship Room. Sinks were added, plus a stove. It served double duty as a workspace for the older women and their circles. Up until then they had to climb the stairs to the all-purpose room upstairs. The upstairs room was fitted out as an open classroom for grades one to six. The two small rooms, including the minister's study, were made into a preschool classroom. The minister took over the very large nursery downstairs and it was made into the biggest and best minister's office in town. Next door to it, with a connecting door, the former high school classroom was made into the secretary's office. Jennie and I enjoyed assisting with the painting and similar work that needed to be done. Volunteer help from the congregation did the heavy work of tearing down walls. At the beginning Jennie, as the new head of the Sunday school, held services downstairs in the dining room for the remaining eight children, as a single class. We called it "Junior Church." Both of us were state certified public school teachers so that we were professionally qualified for the work before us. We recruited a few wonderful teachers when we started with the open classroom. We gradually increased the attendance over the next three or four years to about thirty children. It was one of the most rewarding jobs I ever participated in. Incidentally, I taught the preschoolers while Jennie managed the six classes in the open classroom with the other teachers.

The day finally arrived when our minister retired. Jennie and I were also getting older. With me in my eighties and Jennie in her seventies, we had to turn our jobs over to younger people. The teacher taking Jennie's place was pretty good and kept the Sunday school operating very well.

The 1990s opened up a new era in our lives. Neither one of us ever stopped learning and gaining new knowledge. We were both avid seekers of the truth in this world.

Jennie had read the Bible through, cover to cover, ten times over a period of about ten years. The eleventh time she decided to record all of the women mentioned in it, noting their names and any special features and positions of each one. She may have omitted a dozen or so, but only because it was sometimes very difficult to detect whether some of those Hebrew names were male or female. I helped her with designing and arranging a pamphlet listing them. We printed and copyrighted it as "Biblical Women" and distributed it the best we could.

We also took time to learn about the Dead Sea Scrolls that came into the possession of an American cleric and the head of the Jewish Intelligence Service during the Seven Days War in 1967. They got the Jewish Army to raid a Moslem shop on the outskirts of Jerusalem and confiscate them. The Moslem owner had obtained them for pennies from the shepherds that discovered them in some of the caves around Qumran, the Essene capital city at the head of the Dead Sea, holding out for a higher price. They later rewarded the owner with a handsome price but not as much as he wanted.

Incidentally, one of these caves was the birthplace of Jesus in what is said to be 7 BC. They are just a short distance outside of the city limits of Qumran. The Jewish government keeps the scrolls in their government library. Any valid scholar can read them and take notes but they cannot be removed from the library.

Dr. Barbara Thiering, who has a doctorate in theology, was a professor in the School of Theology at the University of Sydney. She studied and took notes on the Scrolls for twenty years. She is one of the two greatest experts in the world in the Hebrew and Greek languages and the Dead Sea Scrolls. She wrote a book, *Jesus the Man*, describing the amazing story of that first century of Judaic Christianity. I have the book. I studied it and compiled a pamphlet recording a blow by blow description of that Crucifixion Passover. I had her permission to make up the pamphlet and I sent her a copy of it.

Dr. Thiering also translated the Book of Revelation, which contains a history of many of the important events up to AD 114. Written in Pesher style, it substitutes nicknames for real people, real places and real events. We do the same things today when we talk about the Lions, the Colts, the Jaguars and thousands of other people, places and things. We do not take our nicknames literally because we know the truth. But when most of our Christians read the same kind of stuff in the Bible, they take those words literally.

Her book on Revelation is called *Jesus of the Apocalypse.* Doubleday in Sydney and London publishes it, but some of our churches have prevented it from being published in America yet. I have a copy that a dear friend of ours sent us from London, so I was able to study the book thoroughly and compiled two pamphlets on it, which I also sent to Dr. Thiering. One of my pamphlets is 'The Four Horsemen." I recorded the entire twelve verses in Chapter 6, in which the writer, John Aquila of Zebedee, describes the introduction to the people of the first formal New Testament. King Agrippa II, Roman Christian, authorized it. The project was executed by Matthew, the then priest-pope at Ephesus. At that time Jesus was in the Essenes' headquarters in Rome and Matthew recalled Jesus to Ephesus to help with the procedure. This all happened in A.D. 49-50. My other pamphlet was a compilation of two or three verses from each of the twenty-two chapters in Revelation, giving Dr. Thiering's translation of each verse. I distributed my story of the Four Horsemen—(Plus 2) to about one hundred and fifty ministers in the entire area around Geneva, Elmira, Corning and Horseheads, New York. I got answers from only four of them. But I am certain that I shook up a lot of them. The truth is a serious threat to their jobs.

* * *

In the late 1990s, Jennie's health deteriorated. In January 1996 she had emergency surgery and we discovered that she had cancer on her intestines and she ended up with a colostomy bag. Her ovaries were removed and were found to be cancerous, very far advanced. A year of chemotherapy brought the cancer down but it would not stay down. Jennie chose not to continue chemotherapy, which would have been necessary for the rest her life. One year was wicked enough. She chose alternative health procedures, which failed. She died December 3, 1997—five months short of our golden wedding anniversary. We served each other completely for fifty years. Jennie and I had never had any regrets for the past including the failures. We always lived close to God and close to each other.

We also always helped anyone that God put in our path to help. We have never been afraid to live and we have never been afraid to die. I hope that reciting my life experiences gives you some inspiration for improving and enjoying your own life experiences.

Cmdr. Donald O. Burling, USNR

From his official Naval records

Born November 20, 1901 in New London, Connecticut, Donald O. Burling had an extraordinary service record in addition to his many talents and scholarly interests.

His record of service taken from his honorable discharge papers from the Navy. His release from active duty with an honorable discharge from the Official Separation Center, Boston, Massachusetts, May 30, 1946, as Donald 0. Burling, commander of the United States Navy. At the time of his discharge he was married and living in Dorchester, (Norfolk) Massachusetts.

His Record of Naval service shows he enlisted April 1919 and was commissioned in February 1926. His date of entry to active service was October 29, 1940 and his place of entry into active service was Springfield, Massachusetts. His qualifications and certificates held were command AK and executive on AD and executive on AP. He completed four years at the United States Naval Academy in 1925. His off-duty educational courses completed were seamanship core and gunnery core. He served on the following vessels and stations:

Recruiting, Springfield, Massachusetts; USS *West Point*; USS *President Monroe*; USS *Cascade* (AD 16) and the USS *Vega*, (AK

17). He received these honorable: the American Defense Ribbon (A), American Theater Ribbon, European Theater Ribbon, Asiatic Pacific Ribbon (one star). His total payment at time of discharge was $562.17. His required insurance premium amount due each month was $8.50.

His last employer before active duty was the New England Tel & Tel Company, Lancaster, New Hampshire, from June 1926 to October 1940. His main civilian occupation was commercial manager of business offices.

The route of wartime service was from October 1940 to May 1946. He was called to active duty October 1940 from Lancaster, New Hampshire, to Springfield, Massachusetts. Then to Newport, Rhode Island, Norfolk, Virginia, to the USS *West Point*, troopship, 6,000 troops. As troop management officer Donald Burling started his sea duty, which spanned over the next five years of his life. He saw the following ports: New York, Lisbon, Norfolk, Halifax, Trinidad, Cape Town, Bombay, Singapore, Colombo, Bombay, Aden, Suez, Perth, Adelaide, Melbourne, Wellington, San Francisco, Wellington, Melbourne, Wellington, Panama, Colon, New York, Halifax, Liverpool, Glasgow, New York, Rio de Janeiro, Bombay, Melbourne, Wellington, Auckland, Noumea, Brisbane, Melbourne, Auckland, San Francisco, Wellington, Melbourne, Bombay, Suez, Massaua, Aden, Rio de Janeiro, New York, Casablanca, Boston, San Francisco.

He went to Portland, Oregon, to the USS *President Monroe* as executive officer. The troopship had 5,000 troops, and traveled to Seattle, Kodiak, Dutch Harbor, Adak, Dutch Harbor, Kiska, Honolulu, San Francisco. Then to Honolulu to the USS *Cascade*, destroyer tender a floating Navy yard where he served as executive officer. He serviced destroyers on the Western Pacific drive. This commission took him to Funafuti, Kwajalein, Majuro, Kwajalein, Eniwetok, Ulithi, Guam, and Ulithi. Then to the USS *Vega* as commanding officer of an engineering ship with a company of

Sea Bees. He sailed to San Diego, Los Angeles, San Francisco and to the ship graveyard to decommission the ship.

January 1946 Donald Burling went to Boston, Massachusetts. He went on a four-month accumulated leave and detached from active duty, May 1946.

United States Naval Academy

When Donald O. Burling graduated from the U.S. Naval Academy, June 1925, it was a special occasion for several reasons. He received the Newhall prize and was given a $100 bond. And he was handed his diploma by President Calvin Coolidge, who addressed the ensigns. Coolidge's remarks are interesting in hindsight.

On June 4, the *Baltimore Sun* printed an account of President Coolidge's remarks to the Naval Academy. The headlines on the front page, above a photo, read: PRESIDENT COOLIDGE DELIVERING DIPLOMAS TO NEWLY COMMISSIONED ENSIGNS AT NAVAL ACADEMY.

Under the photo was printed "Scene in Dahlgren Hall, Naval Academy, as midshipmen receive their reward for four years of faithful work from the hand of their commander-in-chief the President of the United States."

The article reads as follows (still describing photo): With the diplomas, which signify a task well done, go commissions as ensigns in the United States Navy or as lieutenants in the Marine Corps. There were 448 graduates. Secretary Wilbur, in civilian clothes, on extreme left. Governor Ritchie, in black coat with flower in buttonhole, is above the President.

The J. F. Essary's article proclaimed in a story headline: Coolidge Finds No Country Foe of This Nation / Tells Navy Graduates It is "Very Serious" To insinuate Contrariwise / Opposes Extensive Force as Menace Governor Ritchie Among Notables at Annapolis' Annual Ceremonies.

"President Coolidge, in an address before the graduating class of the Naval Academy today, sought to banish from the minds of the young officers and of the country that Japan or any other nation harbors hostile intent toward America. He said that, although he regarded the navy as a powerful instrument for peace, he believes firmly in maintaining a military and naval establishment formidable enough to guarantee the nation's security, promising adequate support of the American people for such a force.

"At that, the President wanted it understood that he takes no stock in the suggestion for an armed force on this continent so powerful that no possible enemy would dare to make an attack. 'I know of no nation in history that has ever been able to attain that position,' he said. 'I see no reason to expect that we could be the exception.'"

The president added that "peace is an adventure in faith" and that "we must call into action the spiritual and moral forces of mankind."

After the ensigns received their commissions and received their epaulettes the *Sun* reported, "Outside proud mothers, sweethearts and sisters were kept busy fastening the gold and blue insignias upon the shoulders of new officers. Some of them were rewarded with kisses."

The Soldier's Background

Jennie's ancestors

One day I was looking through a drawer in a highboy for something else and found two slips of paper with these notes written by my wife, Jennie's, grandmother (for whom she was named, and in whose home she was born, in Middlesex). Her name was Jennie Lane.

Jennie never told me about her ancestors, but I did some research in the *Chambers Biographical Dictionary* and found that Israel Putnam was one of our early great generals (1718–1790). Born in Salem Village, now Danvers, Massachusetts, on January 7, 1718, in 1740 he started life as a farmer. In 1755 he was a captain repelling a French invasion of New York, and served at the battle of Lake George. In 1759 he commanded a regiment; his rank was lieutenant colonel. In 1764 he helped to relieve Detroit, being besieged by Pontiac. A militant patriot who went to the battles of Lexington and Concord, in 1775 he commanded the forces of Connecticut. He was first a brigadier, then a major general when he helped to fortify Breed's Hill. He served at Bunker Hill. Later he served in defense of the Highlands of the Hudson. He was in command of New York City until George Washington arrived in April 1776. In addition, he served in some of the Indian wars.

Jennie never boasted about anything that showed her as important. She never told me about her being a direct descendant of General Putnam, who was the great-grandfather of Jennie's grandmother, Jennie Lane. Jennie Lane's grandmother was Ann Putnam, one of Putnam's two daughters.

Jennie's fighting spirit

When Jennie was in high school, near the end of her senior year, the Regents exams were about to begin. Jennie arrived at the classroom a bit late. The teacher in charge told Jennie that there was only one seat left. The seat was number thirteen. Nobody would take it, except for Jennie. Her spirit has always been the same as that of Admiral Farragut, in his winning the Battle of Mobile Bay, down in the New Orleans area. When he was advised of the danger of torpedoes from the Confederate gunboats, Farragut roared out with "Damn those torpedoes! Full speed ahead!" Jennie passed the exam. This was just one small incident for Jennie. But she lived her whole life like this—every day.

Jennie, the nurse and scholar

Jennie Calhoon Burling was a Biblical scholar for more than forty years. She was born at her grandparents' home in Middlesex, New York, on December 23, 1909. Her parents' home was in Penn Yan, New York, located on Keuka Lake, one of the Finger Lakes. Jennie graduated from Penn Yan Academy in 1930, then attended Clifton Springs Sanitarium and Clinic School of Nursing, graduating in 1933 as a registered nurse. She then returned to Penn Yan to work at the Soldiers and Sailors Hospital. Several years later she joined the Army.

In 1941 she was called by the Red Cross to serve her country in the Army Nurse Corps. Her assignment for overseas duty was a Station Hospital in Iran as a chief nurse. She met me on board the troop ship carrying her to Bombay. After a long tour of duty in Iran, she returned to the States and was assigned to a military general hospital at Butler, Pennsylvania. After the signing of the

Peace Treaty, she was discharged from military service with the rank of captain and returned to her home in Penn Yan, where she rejoined the staff of the local hospital. I wrote to her and proposed, and nine months later we were married.

Jennie was often called upon to speak before various community groups and service clubs in Butler about her experiences as a nurse in Iran.

Her notes, reproduced here, describe some of the experiences during her long period of duty in Iran, where the allies carried out a gigantic medical and materials service to support the Russian front. Upon her return to the States after the war Jennie was assigned duty at the Deshon General Army Hospital in Butler. Her chief nurse sent her to these various local organizations in a publicity endeavor for these people. I left her words as near to her own writing with some minor edits. After all, these were personal notes used for several superbly delivered speeches in the area. Jennie devoted herself to a lifetime of commitment in every position she was placed in during her years of nursing service until her death. She wrote:

> On December 11, 1942, at dawn, it was a cold, damp, misty morning as our ship eased into dock at Khorramshahr, Iran, with its first troops for the Persian Gulf command. The task before the Command was to deliver American Supplies across Iran to the hard-pressed Russians. Working in unbelievable climate and country and against inconceivable difficulties, they delivered in record time, 4,500,000 long tons of every thing a fighting people needed. Iran is one of the oldest countries of the world, often spoken of as the Cradle of Civilization. Three large rivers flow into the Gulf the Tigris, the Euphrates, which joins 10 miles above the city of Basra and forms the Shatt Al-Arab and the Karum, which flows in from the east at Khorramshahr, five miles below Basra. The land is absolutely flat with numberless streams. Date palms cover the banks but do not extend very far inland because they need irrigation. For 345 days in the year the sun shines and in the summer sends the thermometer up to 140 degrees Fahrenheit in the shade.

It is sometimes so hot that you will raise a blister if you take hold of a steel tool lying in the sun. Rains fall only in the winter, middle of December to the first part of April. It never snows yet on the high mountains to the east snow can be seen in winter. Both the winter and summer are uncomfortable the winter because of its chilly dampness and the summer because of its steamy heat. The great storyteller, Marco Polo, claimed that his sword melted in its sheath when he reached Basra.

The people are mostly Arabs. People whose ancestors came from the Arabian Dessert and conquered the Gulf area 1,300 years ago were a tough breed. The natives migrate, spending the summer in the mountains and the winter in the low country. They have a reputation for plundering caravans, kidnapping foreigners, and extracting the last penny in a business deal.

Because of a lack of water and a distance from the rivers, much rich land is unusable and the people are very poor. Normally day laborers receive about fifteen cents per day and *skilled* labor is not over fifty cents. For protection against brigands and to be near water the people live in villages and cities where the houses are crowded together with narrow alleys for streets. Houses usually contain no furniture. People eat and sleep on the floor. In the cities poverty is obvious everywhere, but there are a few officials, merchants and landlords whose income allow comfortable and even luxurious living.

The Near East has no sanitation, as we know it. In the villages, animal dung is plastered on the house walls to dry and then used as fuel for cooking. Houses have no toilets or latrines. Any open space is used and most often the area around the village or wall is the public toilet. Water is so scarce that the few streams are used in washing the dead, laundering the clothes, bathing the babies and also for drinking. Because people live in constant contact with the animals, fleas, bedbugs, body lice and other insects abound. Sheep and camel ticks (carriers of spotted fever) crawl from the stables which are usually attached to the house, or actually inside it. Trachoma, a dangerous eye disease, causes much blindness. Skin and intestinal diseases were ever present. Only in the cities is any effort made to prevent and cure disease. The penetrating and burning rays of the

sun are the only disinfectant for most people. Having told
you a little about the country I will proceed with our
adventure in the far off country. We were taken from the
ship to our temporary quarters by British ambulances. Our
quarters were on an old hospital barge anchored on the
Karum river six feet from shore. Here on this river we saw
the ancient and modern ship lay side by side.

Very shortly after our arrival the native women began to
arrive at the river banks, to wash their clothes, dishes,
bathing and to fill jars with drinking water. The Moslems
believe that all running water is pure. The men would come
early in the morning and sit for hours watching us. The
nights were cold and damp on the river. We had no heat.
We depended upon Mother Nature for our heat. All win-
dows and doors were open to allow the sun's heat to pen-
etrate the interior. Four PM the barge was closed in order to
retain the heat of the day. To have warm water for bathing
and laundering we filled our steel helmets and placed them
in the sun for one half-hour. The first three days our diet
consisted of tea, thick slices of British bread, and jam for
breakfast. The same for lunch and supper with mutton or
turnips added. There was only a two-burner oil stove for
cooking and boiling our drinking water. One day an Officer
took a group of nurses to a bazaar in Basar. The next day
the Officer's English-speaking houseboy told him that the
shopkeepers in Basar considered him wealthy because he
had all of his mistresses dressed alike.

Five days after we had landed the thirtieth was divided.
Half were sent on detached service. Five hours by rail to
Ahwaz. We were ready for almost anything. You can
imagine our surprise when we were met at the station by
modern bus, more surprised when we found warm comfortable quarters waiting for us. Innerspring mattresses, hot
and cold running water. A warm lunch was waiting. There
was soup, coffee and crackers. We went to bed that night
very happy. We at last had a job to do.

Our hospital to be was a two-story concrete building. The
first floor of the hospital was a mess. Polish volunteer
workers were on the second floor caring for all the patients.
In seven months they had been taught enough English to
care for our men. They were mostly civilian men who went
over for construction of the area.

The operating room staff did a wonderful job in redecorating. The corps men found some green and white paint. They mixed some together painting the side walls and ceiling a pale green, the floor the dark green. The home-made table and stands and cupboards painted white. The reflector above the operating room table was a large aluminum-mixing bowl turned upside down. It was polished to a high luster with a cluster of bulbs in the center. All wrappers, drapes, etc., had to be made. Sometimes the corps men would take the needle and do a little sewing. One of the corps men made a wire frame for a glass jar fastened a string to a foot pedal, punched holes in the top and we had a soap dispenser when scrubbing. Our autoclave was similar to a steam pressure cooker. Steam was generated by gasoline. When twenty pounds of pressure was obtained, the bundles, dressings, etc., was placed in it for one hour. We had no way of knowing whether the supplies were sterile. We never had a wound infection, which was our only proof.

The nurses on the wards worked just as hard helping to clean the rooms down stairs and preparing them for the surgical cases. Everyone was happy because they were nursing more or less in the primitive state. As far as possible I gave hours off the same as in the states. Therefore the nurses did have an opportunity to see the country. Whenever the nurses were invited on an excursion, a medical officer had to accompany them. We planned a party for the enlisted men Christmas Eve. After that was under way, we gathered in the so-called living room. That evening there were five Polish, British nurses, officers and some of our own officers. We sang songs, visited, then we all went to midnight mass in the hospital. A few days later, the Polish nurses came to me with a bottle of scotch for the nurses in the appreciation of the happiest Christmas in five years. One day I was on a hunting expedition out in the desert. There was an Army truck way out in the desert near a village of mud buildings doling out garbage from the Army mess. They did that rather than bury it and having the natives dig it up and eat it dirt and all. All dwellings are protected with a fairly high wall. This was built before the homes in order to protect their building materials. Stealing is not considered a crime if one isn't caught at it. The more one can steal, the more honor and prestige he obtains in their own little circles. Everyone that has the opportunity to visit the Biblical city of Shush usually takes advantage of it. There, the ruins of Queen Esther's castle can be seen. Some of the huge columns are still lying where they have fallen years ago. A short distance away, on a hill overlooking the once fertile land of this ancient empire, stands the replica of this castle built by the French in 1928. Some of the ancient irrigating ditches still can be seen. Daniel's tomb is also in the city.

Dizifal is believed to be the hottest city in the world and is one of the oldest cities of the world. Some think this to be the city of rats spoken of in the Bible. As a home crumbles a new home is built on top of the old one. Therefore we find the natives living in caves far below the surface during the winter. After our sight-seeing trip that Sunday we had dinner at a British Officer's Club. As we were eating, a group of officers from Tehran came in and joined us. At nine o'clock I asked my escort to take me home. A lieutenant colonel in the party said you are not taking Miss Calhoon back to Ahwaz tonight. Take her to the field hospital and go early in the morning. I said, "Colonel, what would my nurses think seeing their chief come in at that time of the morning?" My escort took me home. He said very little during that eighty-mile ride as we reached the fork of the road to Folebade and Ahwaz. He stopped the car got out and stretched. He said you don't know it but you have come over the most dangerous road in Iran. We had no protection. We could have been carried to the hills and held for ransom or killed. That is why the colonel didn't want us to return tonight. I was glad to learn the facts afterwards. I don't think I would have enjoyed that trip otherwise.

Late one afternoon I was out on the desert on a hunting expedition. I saw three women carrying a goatskin filled with water. They had been to the river fifteen miles away. All the water that is used in the desert villages has to be transported in that manner. The natives never walk side by side as we do but in a single column four to six feet apart. I visited a bake shop one afternoon; the main food in the desert area is their bread called a *japady*. This is made of flour, little sugar, salt and water. This is mixed in a concrete bowl funnel shaped. After it is mixed the dough is placed on a table where it is cut, kneaded and then baked on the ceilings of concave ovens. The bread is about 1/16 to 1/8 inches thick, and about as large round as our dinner plates. After it is baked the bread is thrown in a huge pile on the floor. Rice and tea is part of their diet. I have seen our native guide pull some grass from the flower beds roll it in his japady and eat it.

As I rode through the back streets of Ahwaz, their ditches were filled with green slimy water and children playing in it and drinking it. Their dead is buried before sundown. One of the cemeteries I have seen, the graves were covered with cement to prevent the wild animals from digging up the dead. When they visit the grave they spread a rug about and it looks like a tea party. The more money a family has the more he can have.

During the summer the nurses who were stationed in the South slept out of doors under a sandfly net. The sand flies were terrible. Being so hot they would wrap themselves in wet sheets. In March 1943 I rejoined my unit as chief nurse in Tehran. The thirty had taken over the Presbyterian Mission Hospital. The hospital was stationed in the city. High mud walls were all around it, with a front gate and a back gate. The Army built seven buildings each containing thirty-three beds. There were trees; flowers just like that back home. Our water came from a drilled well of some five hundred feet. Even this had to be chlorinated before we could use it. The nurses lived in homes there on the compound. There were at least two, three and four nurses to a room. The first fires were built under the hot water heater. Our shower was more or less in the center of the room. At first the toilets had to be flushed with a pail of water finally water was piped to the bathroom.

All outward appearances of Tehran looked like a modern city. The main streets were paved and shaded with trees. Street lights, fountains, and flowers. The public buildings were modern showing the German influence. The water supply of the city is obtained from the mountains a few miles away; open ditches from the large open ditches to smaller ones lead to the homes and gardens. There were all type of shops. When a native saw an American coming, up went the prices. One must not be too hasty to buy.

One day Mrs. Dreyfus invited me to lunch with one of the medical officers. I had no idea where I was going until

Captain Able told me that we were going to the American
Legation. I had a sinking feeling. It was my first time but
not the last. One day I asked Mrs. Dreyfus if I might
accompany her to the caves. This was in the slums of
Tehran where she was carrying on social work. One of her
patients was a boy about four feet tall. He had received a
very bad burn on his left leg. When he came to her his leg
was bent up. She dressed the wound stretched the leg a little
and told him to return in three days. When I saw it the leg
was straight. He was walking on it. But it will be a long
time before it will be healed. She was trying to get him in
the Polish Hospital for grafting. She told me about babies
with sores, etc. She then took me to some of their homes; I
have never seen anything like it. A small child lying on the
floor of one home sick with typhus. I saw opium dens where
men and women go to try to forget their suffering.

One Sunday I had dinner with one of the missionary's
family. We were asking if she had any trouble in speaking
the language. She told us this, I was teaching a new
mother's class and telling them that the babies should be
fed barley water (*obwaterjo* barley) I combine the two
words for barley water. The mothers said not objo. I was
insistent until I found out that objo meant beer. That
summer the nurses worked in the outside ward with a
temperature of 125 degrees. The patients lay on their backs
with just the trousers of the pajamas. Coolies would go
through the ward throwing water on the floor and in three-
quarters of an hour the floor would be dry.

With the heat of the day and a high temp of a fever the
patients suffered. When we had a serious case such as hem
smallpox I put specialists on with the patients when I could
spare them. If not, corps men were put on supervised by
nurses. The men were taken care of well as far as supplies
and equipment went. During the summer months I had the
nurses on night duty one week at a time. It was impossible
to sleep and the natives were always noisy. Our work was
generally malaria, colds, pneumonia and sandfly fever.

We had movies five times a week after the six months in
Iran. Supplies were a long time in arriving. The Red Cross
workers arrived five months after the nurses. Dances were
held for the enlisted men. Girls were from the better homes
of Iran and refugees. Sight-seeing tours were arranged. Four

hospitals were built in Iran. After the first year the medical were sent out to other countries. The need for medical personnel was not as great as planned. They had planned ten percent to be ill. Only about four percent were ill. In October 1943 I was transferred to a large hospital which was stationed at Khorramshahr. It took two days on the train to Tehran then to Ahwaz. I rode a diesel engine from Ahwaz to Khorramshahr. The engineer wouldn't let me ride any other way because the train was a freight train. That was an enjoyable trip.

The day had been hot so after the train had cleared the freight yards, I was allowed to go out in front. Then I received the cool evening breeze. The engineer had me autograph his permit for me to ride with him. He told me that it was a red-letter day for him. It was the first Army nurse to ride in the cab with him. He had air all the way in the brakes. As I rode out front I had the full view of the desert. I thought there are always compensations for everything. To forget all the filth and the unpleasant scenes that are witnessed during the day, God gives that country a beauty unequal to any part of the world, and that is in the twilight and early evening. Words cannot describe the majestic beauty of the heavens as the last shadows of the day creep away giving the silvery moon and the stars the place of honor in the sky of the Middle East. The coloring of the sky is magnificent, and the nights are gorgeous.

* * *

Media coverage

Jennie's talks received excellent—sometimes daily—coverage in the newspapers as can be seen from the following local excerpts:

The headline in the *Daily Times*, Beaver, Pennsylvania, on November 10, 1944, read: ARMY NURSE TO BE SPEAKER AT MEET OF BOOK AND PLAY CLUB

And the story said: "Captain Jennie L. Calhoon of Deshon Hospital, Butler, Pennsylvania, will tell of her work at the hospital. And, of her experiences during a year and a half in Persia when the Rochester Book and Play Club meets at 8 o'clock Tuesday evening in the home of Mrs. John Hunter, Madison Street. The program will be open to guests."

Or again, from the *Daily Times,* November, 11, 1944

CAPTAIN CALHOON OF DESHON HOSPITAL

TO SPEAK TO CLUBWOMEN

Captain Jennie L. Calhoon of Deshon hospital, Butler, will
address the Woman's Club of Freedom at the monthly
meeting, Monday evening, November 13, in the clubrooms.
Mrs. Olive Nelson will be the "Club Commentator." This
will be the occasion of the club's annual covered-dish
dinner scheduled at 6:30 o'clock.

From the *Daily Times*—Beaver, Pennsylvania, November 15,
1944

FREEDOM CLUBWOMEN HEAR ABOUT PERSIA AND DESHON HOSPITAL

Freedom Clubwomen listened to tales of faraway Persia
(Iran), onetime "Cradle of Civilization" as told by Captain
Jennie L. Calhoon of Deshon Hospital, Butler, Monday
evening at the annual covered-dish dinner of the Woman's
Club. Captain Calhoon, who went to Iran with the first unit
of army nurses, spent seventeen months there. She has been
stationed at Deshon hospital about seven months. Persia, a
small country in northern India, strategically located
between the Persian Gulf and the Gulf of Oman on the
South and the Caspian Sea on the north, was for sometime
the main supply line to Russia and for this reason played an
important part in the war during the winter and spring of
1943, the speaker said.

Captain Calhoon said the Iranians looked upon the American nurses as strange creatures, marveling at their mode of
dress and their freedom with their men folk. They had
never seen women walking and talking with men on the
streets, and with their faces uncovered. "The native men
simply shook their heads in amazement as they sat from
morning until night, at first, watching us," she said.

The nurses gave the Iranians, British and Russians a new
impression of the American people as they saw them
working under difficulties in the hospitals, caring for the
wounded and sick. They made many friends among them.
Above everything else, Captain Calhoon said she learned
tolerance.

She spoke, too, of Deshon Hospital, which services ill and
wounded men, returned from overseas, are being treated,
especially in orthopedics and for defective hearing. There

are only a few mental cases at the hospital.

The patients are being helped to help themselves, to adjust themselves either to return to duty or for civilian life. They are taught lipreading, fitted with hearing aids and are instructed in occupational physiotherapy, learning arts and crafts. She told of the social activities and entertainment provided there for them and of their splendid response. "They have that American spirit—the spirit of going ahead no matter how difficult the going," she said in closing.

Mrs. Clifford N. Robinson, program chairman, introduced the speaker. She announced that the club's annual Christmas dinner would be held December 1 in the Presbyterian Church, when Marian Foster Smith of Saxonburg, will read poetry.

The *Daily Times*, November 16, 1944 Clubs—Society News

BOOK AND PLAY CLUB HEARS ARMY NURSE AT ROCHESTER:

PROGRAMS ARE ANNOUNCED

Capt. Jennie L. Calhoon, Deshon Hospital nurse, addressed the Rochester Book and Play Club and their guests at a meeting in the home of Mrs. John W. Hunter, Rochester, Tuesday evening. Captain Calhoon told of many incidents of her work in Persia, where she served seventeen months as a nurse before going to Deshon hospital, where she has been stationed seven months. An open forum followed her talk.

And she was pictured during an historic event on Tuesday, May 1, 1962

All Eyes on Bruce First graders at Braintree, Massachusetts school watch closely as little Bruce Turner bravely takes first drink of oral polio vaccine. He was first in Massachusetts to take part in statewide test. Vaccine given by Nurse Jennie Burling (AP Wirephoto)

* * *

Our relationship was special even before our marriage, as you can see from this letter from Jennie to me in 1947, a year before our marriage on May 8, 1948. I have saved this letter for more than fifty years. Madeline was chief nurse of Jennie's unit. She was the one who persuaded Jennie to join the Red Cross and put her name on the volunteer list for Army service. She is also the person who introduced Jennie to me on the USS *West Point*. When they ended up in Tehran the unit was divided in half, with Jennie being assigned to Ahwaz as chief nurse.

Bill (who is mentioned in her letter below) was a very good pharmacist. After buying the pharmacy in Elmira and running it for several years, he sold it. Jennie got back every cent that she had loaned him.

My Darling Don,

Sorry you are unable to visit Albany. Maybe some time in the near future. I wish it were possible for you to spend a weekend here to meet Mother and Dad even though we would have very little time to discuss our own problems. Do you think it could be arranged some time in the near future. They are very anxious to meet you.

In my last letter I told you that I was seeing the president of the Board of Managers, as yet, I have not. If all goes well I will tomorrow. He has been very busy with the campaign in raising $150,000 for a new wing to the hospital and he has spent very little time here.

This has been a dark rainy Sunday. I had 12:30 to 3:30 off and spent that time in listening to the radio and dreaming. I spend nearly all of my free time in my room just to think and plan, whether it will get me anywhere time will tell.

Here comes more questions; do you have a car? On what floor is your apartment and how many rooms do you have? Do the rooms have good light, what type of heat do you have? How are the hospitals out there, are they all large ones or do you have a few that are small? Is there one near your apartment? Do you know anything about the working conditions, salary, etc.?

Do I understand correctly that if my answer is yes you would be willing to wait to marry in September? Dear Don you may think my questions are very foolish, but some of the answers will mean a lot to me.

Five years ago today you went to chapel with me remember? [On the West Point]. I was greatly surprised to find you waiting for me. Madeline put on her BLUE acts and you went to your room. That girl has caused much unhappiness.

I visited a friend of mine at Valley Forge General Hospital in Pennsylvania during my vacation. I arrived there on Friday. Clara met Madeline in the mess hall and told her I was here. Mad [Jennie's nickname for Madeline] came to my room and awakened me. My greeting was sort of cool. She had just come off from a tour of night duty and was on her way home for the weekend. She looked much older and there was sort of a hard look about her. Funny how fate steps in and changes the course of life for all of us. She wanted to know who I was traveling with and I told her that I was alone. She was amazed that I would be so far away from home alone.

In one of your letters you told me that you knew me better than I did myself. I believe that you have something there. I can assure you that I don't know myself the past month. One day I think I have the answers and the next I don't have. Will I ever settle down and be my old self once again? You invested your life savings in a little store and I have done the very same thing. I hope I don't lose all that I have given. Every one says that the drug store is very nice and that Bill [Jennie's oldest brother] should make a go of it. If it hadn't been for me he never could have gone on his own. It will be a year next March. Bill has increased his stock considerable during the past six months. Ruth his wife works the soda fountain with the aide of their daughter who will be eighteen next May. Just think I have been an aunt for eighteen years.

Well my darling it is almost supper time. Then the PM supervisor will relieve me and I will go into my department and get a little work. So far for Monday I have just one case. I have been wondering just what you were doing today and how you spent your time. Do you go to any movies? I haven't been to one since August. While my nephew was visiting here during his vacation he expected his Aunt Jennie to take him on every Tuesday. He is eight years old. I got to wash my hair tonight. I do my own hair. I can't see paying a hairdresser $2.00 every time I went for about one half hour of actual work when I have to work four times harder for my money. I hope that I won't be called out. It is supper time I will say Good night Darling and sweet dreams. Love Jennie

P.S. Home again. Yes darling I do know what hard times are like. Dad has always worked hard. Mother worked

away from home for eighteen years to help buy their home
and to put Bill through College. My school years were
hard. I had most of the housework to do and see that
supper was ready when they came home from work. There
I go contradicting myself about cooking. I haven't done
any cooking to speak of for the past seventeen years.
Mother and Dad would never interfere with us if my
answer is yes. Mother is a very broad-minded individual.
You can ask my sister-in-law. Do you have to keep paying
alimony as long as Flora shall live or is it over a period of a
few years? What hours do you work and what days do you
have off? How long a vacation do you have?

O Darling I wish I could curl up in your arms tonight and
have a nice long chat with you about things. I just don't
know how to express myself on paper. Maybe in some
future date. Good night Darling and may your dreams be
sweet and Happy, Love Jennie

Renewing our vows

Our marriage was very special. On May 8, 1983 we decided, as
many couples do, to renew our vows. The service was written by
our friend and pastor, the Rev. Douglas Passage:

Donald: Will you have this woman to be your wife, and will
you pledge your faith to her, in all love and honor, in all duty and
service, in all faith and tenderness, to live with her, and cherish her
according to the ordinance of God, in the holy bond of marriage?

I will.

Jennie: Will you have this man to be your husband, and will you
pledge your faith to him, in all love and honor, in all duty and service,
in all faith and tenderness, to live with him, and cherish him, according to the ordinance of God, in the holy bond of marriage?

I will.

Please join hands and repeat after me these vows: I, Donald,
take thee Jennie to be my wedded wife and I do promise and
covenant before God and these witnesses to be thy loving and
faithful husband in plenty and in want, in joy and in sorrow, in
sickness and in health, as long as we both shall live.

I, Jennie, take thee Donald to be my wedded husband and I do promise and covenant before God and these witnesses to be thy loving and faithful wife in plenty and in want, in joy and in sorrow, in sickness and in health, as long as we both shall live.

* * *

Declaration: Since you have reaffirmed your love for each other, and before God and these witnesses have exchanged these solemn and joyous vows, as a minister of the Gospel of Jesus Christ, I pray God's continued blessing upon you as husband and wife, Donald Oscar Burling and Jennie Calhoon Burling. What God has joined together, let no one put asunder. May these words of the great apostle continue to be your guide: Love is patient and kind; it is not jealous or conceited or proud; love is not ill-mannered or selfish or irritable; love does not keep a record of wrongs; love is not happy with evil, but is happy with the truth. Love never gives up; and its faith, hope, and patience never fail. Love is eternal.

Prayer: Most merciful and gracious God, of whom the whole family in heaven and earth is named: bestow upon Donald and Jennie the seal of your approval, and Your fatherly benediction, granting unto them grace to fulfill, with pure and steadfast devotion, the vow and covenant now renewed. Guide them together, we beseech You, in the way of righteousness and peace, that loving and serving You with one heart and mind, all the days of their life, they may be abundantly enriched with the tokens of Your everlasting favor. In Jesus' name we pray, Amen.

Let us now sing together "O Jesus, I Have Promised."

Part III

Essays and Poems

by Donald O. Burling

Editor's note: To read his works is to appreciate the man. Donald O. Burling is a prolific author and scholar, writing in prose and poetry on a variety of subjects.

Two Victories
(1916-1917)

In the early part of the century elocution (public speaking) was very popular. At Good Will we had an annual contest for the high school, with a first prize of $5 and second prize of $3. I entered the contest in my freshman year.

I went to my English teacher, Ray Tobey, to help me select a speech. He was in charge of our Carnegie Library, which we had on our school premises. He pulled a big book down from the shelf and turned to a speech delivered by Emile Zola, the great French philosopher.

The time was around 1894, when anti-Semitic activity was running high in France. The speech was given in defense of Captain Alfred Dreyfus, Jewish officer in the French Army, who had been wrongly accused by a strong segment of the Army stealing secret documents and giving them to another country. The sole purpose was to keep Jews out of the French Army.

Dreyfus had been convicted on false testimony and there was a great uproar for his release. Zola was one of the main important people calling for his release. He did get a new trial, and was convicted again. He was pardoned immediately. The officer who gave the false testimony committed suicide. In 1906 the verdict was officially overturned. Dreyfus served in World War I and won the French Legion of Merit award, an equivalent of our Medal of

Honor. I condensed the speech to ten minutes. The officials preferred a five-minute limit, but I needed at least that much to get in all of the essentials. My cottage matron let me use her private side porch to practice the speech.

In the late spring the contest took place in our church on the grounds, serving all of the children and employees on both the boys' farm and the girls' farm two miles up the road. We had our own large church, a regular full size Carnegie Library, a Moody School building, a big administration building built by Prescott, the big shoe polish millionaire, eleven boys' cottages (fifteen to a cottage), three girls cottages, our own water pump station, and a complete farm and dairy layout.

Wealthy organizations and individuals financed all. To this day I do not know the faith of the minister who operated the farm and school. I know that the Fifth Avenue Presbyterian Church sent me to the school through their mission on the East Side in New York City. In the contest the favorite was a senior. The judges could not decide whether to call the senior the winner or me. So they called it a tie. They added first and second prizes together and gave us both one half.

In my sophomore year the school sent me to Skowhegan to represent our school in an annual festival put on in the Skowhegan Opera House for all of the high schools in the Kennebec Valley, from Skowhegan down to Waterville and a little beyond.

The two main events in this festival were a gigantic chorus of voices from all schools, I think over one hundred voices. There was a big grandstand on the stage. The other major event was the elocution contest.

My coach was the wife of our high school principal. The favorite in the contest was a Skowhegan senior. My coach sent me out at my turn to speak. As I got ready to start my speech I saw two students coming down the grandstand. It was really their turn to give their duet. I waved to the audience and got off of the stage as fast as I could. In the offstage waiting room my coach thought I was upset. But I was not upset. They tried to calm me down. I was just mad. I was just getting ready to go out. I was all fired up with all fire and brimstone in defense of Captain Dreyfus.

When the duet finished. I went out on stage. The audience rose and gave me a great ovation. It took a little while before things calmed down and I could start my speech. When I did start, I really gave them all of the hell and brimstone that Zola had in his original speech. The audience repeated their big ovation. When the judges came in with their verdict, the kid in knee breeches and long stockings, from the small high school of one hundred students, won the verdict over the favored senior at Skoweghan high school. It was a wonderful victory.

The Bible versus Horatio Alger (1913)

I was in the sixth grade. The teacher ran a little contest over a period of time, posting gold stars on a chart of the student's names, representing excellence in various programs. I won the contest.

The teacher presented me with a book of Bible stories. She later asked me how I liked the book. Shooting from the hip with the truth, like I have done so often in my life, I said to her: "I liked the story very much, but I would have preferred a book of Horatio Alger." Alger's books were popular in those days, reciting tales of poor boys who beat the odds and became rich. Incidentally, I am still a poor boy.

One More Victory (1925)

At the Naval Academy during first class year (senior) there were several honor winners in various areas. The Navy Special Order No. 42-25 listed eleven, including my name. Two of the awards were for the same person, Harry Hubbard, who stood number one in the class. I was number fifty six in our class of 448. Fairly bright, but far from the brightest. God has always found a way to hold my ego down to ground level.

My prize was the Newhall Prize, a $100 bond. A big insurance firm in Philadelphia gave it. It was one of two essay prizes. The boy who won the other prize was William Gallery. He was in my company, living on the same floor in Bancroft Hall and a close friend. He came down to my room, asking for advice as to how to treat the problem, knowing that I was a pretty good writer.

I told him to lean heavily on patriotism, as that was the nature of that essay. I leaned heavily on thrift, savings and insurance, as an insurance company ran my contest. Each of us was competing in only one contest thus concentrating our entire effort on the one job. Ernest Eller, who was also in our company, was by far the best writer in our class.

He entered both contests. He came in second in both contests. I am convinced that if he had concentrated on only one contest that he would have beaten either Bill Gallery or myself.

At the Naval Academy, as at most military schools, the regiment was organized with a midshipman captain in command, and varying officer grades down the line. Those men wore swords and belts. The rest of the men carried only a Springfield rifle. I was the only man in that lineup carrying only a rifle, with a corporal's badge on my arm.

Each company was under the supervision and authority of a regular officer. The one in charge of my company was Lieutenant Connolly. I was never a perfect emblem of discipline and received many demerits for breaking regulations. Mr. Connolly gave me a lot of demerits. I deserved all of them. While most other men were busy at sports, reading, exercising, or just loafing, from 4:00 P.M. to 6:00 P.M. supper time, I was parading on Farragut Field with a rifle on my shoulders, paying off my demerits. But, I respected and loved Mr. Connolly very much. Lieutenant Connolly, knowing me very well was standing, with other officers, near where our honor line was lined up. He came over to me, and asked me, "How did you get up here?" Again, with my terrible habit of shooting from the hip without thinking, I said, "Mr. Connolly, you can't keep a good man down." I wish that I had never said that, but it was the truth.

A Can of Pears (1945)

While serving on the USS *Vega* as commanding officer, I presided at a mast for one of the sailors. Mast is a low court proceeding that takes place on board ship, for the handling of infractions of regulations. It is similar to a village court in a small town. The commanding officer is the judge. He has the authority to dole out small punishments for minor offenses, or pass serious cases on to a formal court-martial.

A Negro boy, serving as a mess attendant, was brought before me by one of my junior officers. He was an officer who was a Southerner who did not like Negroes. The boy had stolen a can of pears from the ship's storage, and the officer asked me to give him a court-martial.

My mother was a Southerner. Her family were born and raised in North Carolina since early colonial days in the 1600s. Some families owned plantations and slaves. Like most plantation owners they treated their slaves well. They had warm, comfortable housing, warm clothing, good food and kind treatment. Those who could handle it were given education as far as they could go.

One of my relations had slaves who were driven north by General Sherman. After the war they returned to my relative and begged him to take them back, just as they used to be. When they were dumped off the train up north, they got no food, no clothing, no housing and no job.

The underground layouts run by many kind people helped a lot of them. Lincoln helped none of them. My relations could not help them. Sherman had destroyed so much that he was just able to survive as a roadside farmer. That was the widespread story of the freedom of the slaves, just freedom period.

I had to give the boy some punishment, as he had really stolen a twenty-five-cent can of pears. So I sentenced him to three days of bread and water, a standard sentence. I did not follow up to see that the sentence was carried out. I knew as a former enlisted man myself, his buddies would take care of his food problem.

Anatomy of Prayer

The story of prayer is one of the most intriguing problems in human history. Most human beings realize that God, in many different forms and methods, created us children. Our mothers produced us, and then we communicated with our mothers. But as we grow older, we began to realize that God, in whatever form each religion believes, created all of us in the first place. But how do we communicate with God?

Where are these children, who need a communication system with God? On our planet Earth? Partly. But we are only about five percent of all of His human children. Are you amazed? I was. But let me explore the actual factual history of at least one other planet of habitation in our own Universe. Anyone can check it out with a visit to the nearest bookstore. The time was July 2nd or 3rd, 1947. There is sane disagreement on the actual date. The chief performer was Lt. Gen. Arthur Trudeau, director of Army R & D and manager of a 3,000-plus man operation with lots of projects. He was previously head of Army Intelligence. Lt. Col. Philip Corso was his top assistant on both jobs.

The event was the crash, in Roswell, New Mexico, of an alien scout plane against a mountain side, in a very violent lightning storm. The Army covered the area immediately with troops and imposed secrecy. Many townspeople knew the score, but very little information ever got out to the rest of the country.

The plane was moved away from the crash site on a large Ford flatbed truck. The four crewmen were removed to the hospital at Fort Bliss, with three dead and the skipper nearly dead. The area was covered and searched thoroughly by troops, and all fragments were picked up.

Inspection of all materials and apparatus discovered on the plane was entrusted to General Trudeau. Here I will shift to Fort Riley in Kansas to bring Lieutenant Colonel Corso into the drama.

On July 6, 1947, Lieutenant Colonel Corso was on post duty at night. Earlier in his tour of duty, Corso had joined the fort bowling team as an officer representative and also star bowler. He and a Sergeant Brown, leader of the team, became close friends. That night Brown was on guard duty at an old veterinarian building as head of the guard detail. Brown stopped Corso and told him to go inside and see what was in there. Brown stayed outside on guard. Corso went in with his flashlight. There were four, four-foot caskets, plain cases. One had the securing nails loosened, and Corso easily forced the cover open.

Inside, lying in special liquid preservative fluid, was the four-foot body of one of the flyers. The features were different from ours, with an extra large head, but actually human; their bodies were created by God to be adaptable to the different environment on their planet. The four caskets were en route to Walter Reed Hospital for complete autopsies.

Colonel Corso wrote the complete story in his book *The Day After Roswell*, published by Pocket Books. I recite this brief excerpt from his book for the primary purpose of proving that we have real, factual evidence of the existence of other human beings on at least one other planet in our own Universe. The most amazing fact of this crash is that these people are one giant step ahead of us in technology. But now we have learned much of this technology from them. There is much more in process of being learned. Some of the secrets discovered on the crashed plane and developed by the research groups of major defense contractors were:

The accelerated particle beam, found in nature in:

The lightning bolt

The laser cutting tool

The stealth bomber

The microwave oven

The integrated circuit chip

The Kevlar bulletproof vest

The antimissile missile

The fiber-optic circuit

It is remarkable what a gigantic amount of wonderful blessings those four dead astronauts from Venus gave to us in the crash of their scout plane that July night in New Mexico. Lieutenant General Trudeau and Lieutenant Colonel Corso engineered the entire transition through parceling out each item to the contractor research layouts best qualified for each item.

I mention Venus for this reason.

When Corso looked into the face of the body in the casket at Fort Riley, he saw that the eyes were sunken in slight cavities instead of flush on the face, as are our own eyes on Earth. I deduced that God made them that way to give those people much better protection from the hotter sun on Venus. Besides, in all of the mountains of data sent back to NASA from Mars, there is not one iota of evidence of human life on Mars.

Now we can get down to the very important study of our communication with God in prayer, which is the simplest method of communication available to us.

First, let us try to estimate the number of God's children that are served in all of the universes. We know that there are other neighboring universes that have already been discovered by astronomers. How many more will be discovered? Let us be conservative, and estimate at least a total of ten universes including our own.

We know that our universe has more than five billion people. We know for certain that there is at least one more inhabited planet besides our own in this universe. Let us assume, again conservatively, that each of the other universes has at least two inhabited planets. That makes a total of twenty inhabited planets to be served by God through prayer. And if each of these planets has at least five billion people, that is a total of one hundred billion people to be served by prayer.

How many people still believe that when they pray they are talking directly and personally with God? Please be reasonable. We know from an abundance of personal testimony that many of our prayers are answerable favorably. We also know that many prayers get an unfavorable answer, but they are still answered. Therefore, God is definitely receiving our messages.

We do not know God's definite shape or form, but some of us do believe that there is an unknown multiple entity ruling our universes that we call God for ease of communicating. How does He do it?

Suppose that you have a plumbing disaster in your home. You call a plumber. He is out on a job. You do not hear him, but you still tell him what is wrong, and you need him to fix it. You think nothing of him not being there to hear you personally. You talk to him anyway. You guessed it. You talked to his answering machine. He shows up later at your house and answers your message favorably.

Do you begrudge God using a similar method of communication to serve 100 billion of His children throughout all of His universes? He has a far more elaborate set-up than your plumber, your electrician or any other service that you use.

God probably has a separate answering panel for each planet, as the environment and even the shape and form of His children would vary from planet to planet. Since all of our prayers are sent by voice, He must have a circuit delicate enough and strong enough to carry our voice over many millions of miles to His receiving panel for each planet.

God must have a programming set-up like nothing we humans could ever imagine. Every single request that could be asked connects to an answer, which is activated as soon as the request is received. That would explain how some of our prayers receive an immediate answer.

I hope this brief interlude into God's handling of prayer for *all* of His children will give you some comfort and a lot of pleasure in your future communications with your God. I close this little essay with a story of the closing minutes of a visit of my favorite minister. He always reads, and I think enjoys, much of my writings. Maybe that is why he is my favorite.

One day I told him my view of God's handling of prayer, as I have described herein. Many ministers, at the close of the visit, will rise and hold hands and offer up a closing prayer. When this particular visit ended, Doug [the Rev. Doug Passage] rose, offered his hand and said to me, "Shall we try to get through to God's answering machine?"

I will always love a fan like that.

Two sermons

One of the sermons I delivered from the Pulpit of All Souls Church in Braintree, Massachusetts, when some of the laymen took over the pulpit during the minister's two months summer vacation, circa 1950s.

Lead, Kindly Light

I wonder how often each of us reviews our personal relationship with God, considering what we expect of Him, and what He expects of us? How often do we hold a conference with Him, and of what do these conferences consist? Do we set aside a minute once in a while, or five minutes a day, or an hour each Sunday or is it a continuous sort of thing, keeping Him with us consciously, through all hours and all conditions, good and bad? Do we step into His presence once in awhile, in awe and fear of Him when we need Him real badly, or do we stay in His presence constantly, without fear or awe, but with simple companionship and love to the best of our conception?

It is not difficult to determine what we expect of God. Generally our list of expectations far exceeds the most fantastic Christmas gift lists of our starry-eyed children and it is generally just as unreasonable. But I wonder what God expects of us?

Too many people ask too much of God and thank too little. If God's time were finite, a terrific amount of it would be wasted in listening to our requests for food and riches. Even in the Lord's

Prayer we ask for bread and to be delivered from evil. We ask God not to lead us into temptation. Isn't it a bit queer and ungodly for Him to even think of leading us into evil or temptation?

I have listened to several sermons preached from this pulpit by our higher than average minister in which the underlying message was love. The whole purpose of relationship between God and all creatures is tied to love, not just for God, but between every one of us. God and all of the universes and their contents are infinite. We are infinite and indestructible, also, even though God permits our minds and understanding to develop only to finite boundaries for the time being. All of the apparent evil in the world is only tools for the accomplishment of God's overall program. Since nothing is destructible, the undesirable events in this world will not destroy, but will only serve to increase our knowledge of and companionship with God.

Recently a relative of mine visited her folks in Canada. They are in their eighties. She could not understand why they should be so interested in life. They just laughed at her. Of course they were interested in life, just as much as she, or anyone else. All of the past is gone, if you reason in the finite sense. None of the future has yet arrived. All of us, from the cradle to over one hundred, are living here during this one-day, and life to every one of us is equal as of the moment. If this one moment is lived in usefulness and love, we enjoy it. If it is lived in bias, hate and futile attempts at destruction, we suffer through it. Today, to all of us, is a whole lifetime. Even though it may stretch out for a few years does not make it longer than a day, nor does the shortening of it to an early apparent death make it less than a day. Lived in love, and usefulness, and service, it is a happy day. We do not have to love or serve with perfection. All we have to do is try our best, with the knowledge and equipment which God allots to us.

The service each one gives is not measured in finite amounts. I doubt even if God makes up report cards on us. You either try, or you don't, within the limits of your knowledge. If you don't try enough, perhaps your spirit will have to return time and time again in future mechanical devices called bodies to keep trying until you learn the value and happiness of love. If you do succeed in learning that happiness, you become greater and greater through the wonderful eternal life to which we are so blind because we are so ignorant, and become the Schweitzers and Hoovers and Jeffersons of future periods in this eternal day. We also may become one of the thousands of unknown little people who devote their lives and love and service to just a few people, but give all of it. They are just as great. It is far greater to be a little person in love with your neighbors, than a world leader on a mission of attempted destruction of material or mind of other people.

How can we accomplish this happiness, and fit in knowingly with God's plan of operation of our thousands of universes? You may rest assured that you will fit in with His plan anyway, whether you know or not, or whether you try or not. But to do so knowingly is the ingredient that ferments into happiness. The answer is that all you have to do is try. It doesn't matter how great or how small your success may be. The simplest moron does just as much for God as the greatest scientist. If he tries harder, he does far more than the so-called great man who doesn't try much.

In our conferences with God, why ask for bread, or for the temptation of evil to be taken from in front of us? Why not just ask for knowledge, knowledge of what He wants us to do, knowledge of one more little step that may be right for us to take, just one step at a time. It would avail us nothing to learn of His whole plan at one time, since our tiny, insignificant little earth could neither understand nor profit from it. But for just one step, both our neighbors and we could understand. So for myself I never ask God for bread, or riches or power. I only ask for knowledge. Not knowledge of how to be better than my neighbor, or how to outwit the world, but only knowledge of one more step that God may let me take to serve Him and my neighbors and the universes a little bit better than I did yesterday.

I would not exchange this happiness that I get from my personal relationship with God for all of the riches and power in the world. I know that I will not accomplish much in one short apparent mortal lifetime. This passing phase of our eternal day does not permit tremendous results. But I know that during all of the infinite eternity of which you and I and all peoples and things are part, I will continue to be satisfied with taking one more single, little step as God considers me ready to take each additional step. That is my happiness, and my wealth. It is also yours, if you desire it.

Purpose of Prayer

What is the purpose of prayer? Do you ever keep a list of the prayers that you offer, or perhaps plead, and tally up the things that you discuss with your God? Would you be willing to keep such a record for a month? I think that if you did, you might stop tallying after a week, perhaps sooner, and decide that it was time to reevaluate the whole area of your personal prayer.

What do you say to God? Do you ask for something, some favor or blessing for yourself, or a relative, or a friend? And just what do you accomplish?

We ask for bread, or forgiveness, or success. We even try to pass the buck to God to keep us out of mischief, when that is our own duty. Do we think so little of the power of God, and trust Him so little to do the right thing, that we think the only way to save ourselves is to yell at Him so as to attract His attention, or otherwise He would never know about us or our needs?

Can't we get it through our heads that if God is as powerful, and good, and loving as we suppose Him to be, that He knows our needs, and will fail none that He judges to be necessary, regardless of whether we ask or remain silent. He is our God of love, not hate; our God of understanding and forgiveness, not vengeance; our God of companionship, not fear and aloofness.

Suppose we try a new kind of experiment, a fantastic experiment. Suppose we try trusting our God for just a week. I know that seems a short time for most things, but for this, and for most people, it could be almost an eternity. We are so used to haranguing our God with pleadings and alarms, expecting neat little packages to be delivered to us in solution of the troubles which we put aside as God's duty, so that our own time might be made free for more important things, such as trying to outdo our neighbors.

How can we judge the purpose and the power of prayer, unless we know our God? Is He all powerful, or does He have limitations? This is not an idle question. The very fact that you ask favors of Him, in the imperfect oral language of humans, shows that you feel that He does not know you, or hear you, or guide you, or love you, unless you use such audible language as is made only for our own type of beings. You know in your heart that He is all powerful, and knows the innermost thoughts of every being in every universe, what is good for us, what is bad for us, and what will be done through eternity, regardless of your requests and still you pray to try to get Him to change His mind about your own pet projects.

If God is as great as all of the Faiths proclaim, is it not presumptuous to ask Him to deliver a loaf of bread to us, when He knows that we need it? And most especially when we already have the loaf of bread in our house, why pour out pleadings for something already in hand? And why ask for forgiveness over and over again by rote? I can understand the human anxiety that asks forgiveness for some specific error, but to pour out a blanket appeal seems rather childish. Why not, instead, go through one day without doing anything which we feel needs forgiveness, and then we could have the extreme pleasure of thanking God for making the day so happy, rather than trying to get Him to blot it off the books. Why not go through one day without courting any evil, instead of begging God to force us back from our deliberate footsteps towards the darkness?

My plea is this: we are all the children of God. It is far happier to live with Him as children live with their father and mother, for God is both Father and Mother. I sometimes think that our language is very cruel in not having a sexless pronoun of affection, which would more accurately fit our God. We have lived long enough these many centuries to learn that He harbors only love, compassion, kindliness, understanding. Vengeance and hate belong only in the earthly vocabulary, and are short-lived mirages in the heavens of time.

Whether we listen to the chemist or the theologian, nothing is ever destroyed. Many times we merely discontinue the use of something precious for a time, but it always survives for the pleasure and happiness of those more willing to understand. If we lift the artificial curtain of fear and hate, we will realize how close God really is to us. We do not even have to reach out to touch Him, for He is always touching us, and all we have to do is be willing to feel His touch. God knows our every need, and He will fulfill all of those needs, which He deems necessary, regardless of our exhortations and beggings. Fortunately, He knows and understands our weaknesses and our fears and no amount of bad judgment on our part will prejudice His actions in standing beside us. But it would be wonderful to spend our hours with Him in companionship, and thanksgiving, and love, and not waste these precious hours in pleadings and arguments.

I do not come before you with clean hands. I have made my own exorbitant share of pleadings with Him in my lifetime. It has taken me a long time to gradually learn to be a happy child, rather than a fretful and complaining one. I have eaten no more or no less bread, because of all my prayers. I have neither gained more any less because of them. But in trying to confine my prayers only to love and understanding, I find that the bread continues to be provided, and the gas tank continues to be filled, but the happiness has increased a hundredfold. And so I pass through one more intermission in our lives with a paraphrasing of the prophet's prayer to my own use:

Our God, only God of all the Universes, Thy will is also our will, if we but listen to our souls. Thy desires are also our desires, if we but open our hearts. Thy urge to turn thine own night into thine own day is also our urge, and we will follow it with our hands nestled in Thine, instead of begging thee to drag us with Thee. We cannot ask thee for naught, for thou knowest our needs before they are born in us: Thou art our need; and in giving us more of Thyself, thou givest us all. Amen.

The End of a Prayer (1971)

I have a standard prayer that I pray to God twice a day—once in early morning and once late at night. It is about twenty minutes long, and covers all the bases. From time to time I delete obsolete items and add new. I have prayed it for several years.

I record here the evening of this prayer:

Dear loving God, we thank you for the wonderful human life experiences that you have given us, and to all of your many children throughout all the ages, trillions of them, to be used in implementing all of your plans and programs.

We especially thank you for giving to Jennie and me our wonderful extra long periods of this human life's experiences. We have done the very best that we know how with this gift. And dear Lord, we do not ask you for anything more after this life.

We do not ask you for any eternal life. Jennie and I are completely reconciled, and content, and happy and thankful for all that you have given to us already. We do not ask you for more. We love you very dearly, dear Lord. We love you very much. Amen.

The Drifters

I

The Man of Disappointment

The heavens in their finest splendor clad,
With not a spot to mar the sunset's glow,
Gave all the beauty to the earth they had,
Till far beyond the hills the sun sank low.
A man sat still, enjoying evening's calm,
And traveled back to days long since gone by
He thought of youth, the cheer of love's soft balm
And then of age, and then he gave a sigh.
When young he had ambitions, high-strung hopes,
He had a goal to gain—set high the pace—
With fire of youth he started up the slopes,
To fame, perhaps, if he could win the race
His life had just begun, he did not know
The river's bend would change the river's flow.

II

Ere long misfortune took him for her own,
And one by one each plan he made fell down,
His hopes in sad array from him had flown,
As fortune on him thus began to frown

The first to leave him was his love, whose heart
He thought belonged to him for years to come,
This first great disappointment cut apart
Ambition from the man once gay now dumb
Oh, Earth! The spirits that you crush to naught,
In bitterness regard thy seeming power,
They never know, for they have never fought
Through trials, that it lasts so short an hour.
This man is nearly through with life on earth,
And not a cloud tried he to change to mirth.

III

The Man of Discontent

Another man is on a different way,
Is drifting by so nearly to the end,
He stopped to rest, and on the ground he lay,
The ground around which flowed the last great bend.

He saw a vision, and he watched with awe—
Before his eyes his youth passed gaily by,
A few sweet memories flashed, and then he saw

A cloud of darkness hovering very nigh;
The darkest memory of the lot approached,
He saw the girl he loved—adored the most
He whispered something, then himself reproached,

For leaving her, to join the lesser host.
He was not satisfied, and this just sent
Him down the road to greater discontent.

IV

All ventures that he started never came
To see success—he dropped them all midstream,
Career he never knew, and neither fame,
He never cared to plan, or work, or dream.

He failed to use the talents that he had,
 He was not satisfied with small success,
 And now with body old, and features sad,

He learns that nothing comes from selfishness.
The vision passes, and he tries to call
His youth, that he may live it through once more,
Those years are wasted now, his life and all

That's left, is cast upon the other shore.
He wanders lonely down the last lone stretch,
A broken spirit, and a broken wretch.

V

The Man of Sin

A storm approaches near the desert sand,
The clouds of dust are bonding to the eyes,
A man, alone upon this stormy strand,
Looks anxiously up towards the treacherous skies.

He sees the end, he knows 'tis time to leave
The world, and all it offers far behind;
He wonders how his life he may retrieve,
A life so filled with sin of every kind.

In youth he chose the road of deviltry,
Destroyed each noble dream he ever had,
To sober life preferred he revelry,

To useful deeds the deeds with evil clad.
And as his life passed by before his sight,
He wished that he had followed in the light.

VI

The man is not advanced in years as yet,
But little past the middle age of life
For everything he did has had regret,
Each wicked work cuts through him like a knife.
The vision grows intense—his victims pass—

The ones he robbed of goods, and some of breath,
He shudders under such a sight. Alas!
A soul so tarnished just before the death
The raging tempest is the living storm,

The desert is the field that's left to him,
The clouds of dust are memories far from warm,

The man, a broken soul, so sad and grim
Oh, Fate! Wilt thou take vengeance on him yet?
Or wilt thou just forgive him, and forget?

VII

The Man of Hypocrisy

The autumn time spreads all its glory round
The harvest, that the summers sun has sent,
The trees have bared their leaves upon the ground,

And splendor stands supreme by Cere's consent.
To one whose better days are in the past,
Whose works God either values or deplores?
The harvest time of life has come at last,

And he must soon depart to other shores.
To him there also comes a vision clear,
And all those years he sees at one quick glance.
Through every one he always had a fear

That he could not succeed by remonstrance
With Fate, to spare him all that he deserved,
For snaring friends, who he should long, have served.

VIII

He always pampered human vanities,
While human praise he took in quick return,
Of all the earth's most sad calamities,

Is he who fools himself, and cannot learn?
Those double souls can never win success,
That what is in the heart will make the man,
The real success is due to nobleness,

That deeds sincere stay always in the van.
He tried to gain his selfish ends on earth,

And make all mortals think he loved their cause,
The face he showed the world was scarcely worth
A covering for his soul, which knew no laws

'Tis long too late for him to live again,
For he has long betrayed the trust of men.

IX

The Man of Faith

The thunder stops, the rain has ceased to fall,
A maze of color forms a bridge on high.
That casts its beauteous magic on us all,

And now confirms the splendor of the sky
The day is nearly done, and many gaze
Off towards the west, and marvel at the sight,
The sun is sending forth its fading rays,

And every moment now it grows less bright.
Among them all, a certain one lies still,
A few about him share his dying hours,
As, like the sun, he fades beyond the hill,
And withers as the prettiest of the flowers.

The task of life is done, and death sounds clear,
In peace he passes by, to life, more dear

X

His life was wrought with kindness to them all,
His creed was faith in God, and faith in man,
Enhanced by many storms, he heard their call,
Gave courage here and there a helping hand.
This one strove on, and won the fight at last,
And now with happy vict'ry at his side,
He thinks of days long since lost in the past,

While mortal life is sinking with the tide.
And gazing out along the path he trod,
He sees a greater road that leads above

To heaven, where, enthroned he sees his God,
And now he knows: Reward of love is love.

Into this road a maze of paths converge,
And from these paths the multitudes emerge.

XI

The Roads Converge

Oh, look, ye men, a brilliant light ahead,
Gives promise of the dawn, a newborn dawn!
Into its sparkling splendor come the dead
From all directions to the light they're drawn.

And now their eyes are opened wide, they see
A road that leads beyond their wondrous sight,
Here every heart thrills through with hope and glee,

And everyone is glad to leave the night.
They linger there to see how much is true,
And marvel at the glorious display
So many paths, so many mortals, too,

A promise of a better, brighter day
Oh, dazzling light that leads to Promised Land!
Oh, spacious road, with room where all may stand!

XII

They Lead to a Great City

The anxious throng did not have far to go,
Before they saw great portals greet the sky,
And in their eyes the piercing rays did glow,
Reminding them of all the glory nigh.

A city rose before their wond'ring eyes,
And stretched afar beyond their human sight,
So vast and unproportion was its size,
So blinding was its ever-shining light.

With awe did some approach the Promised Land?
While others greeted it with happy glee,
A beauteous city on the foreign strand,
Awaited them, and soon they all would be

Within its walls, to share its seeming mirth,
For what they saw was never seen on earth!

XIII

The City

They swarmed within, were greeted by their Host,
And felt His hand, but could not see His face,
But straightway some discerned the Spirit's ghost,
Surmised the end of Life's poor, tragic race.

Great structures barred the quickly moving crowd,
With rich adornments strewn along the way,
The sky was clear with neither sun nor cloud
To furnish light, though all was bright as day.

Majestic streets, whose breadth was infinite
Resounded lightly with their massive tread,
And spaces fair, with charms indefinite,

Received the stricken mass of living dead,
Their first excitement soon subsided, till
The army of the earth was calm and still.

XIV

At length, perceiving no one near, they went
By different routes, to seek a resting place,
But to their gaze no earthly charms were lent,
Nor diamonds, pearls, nor gold, nor metals base.

The buildings housed the very rarest arts,
Not stone, or marble things, or tableaux fair,
But living gems, with beauteous, quivering hearts,
From mortal touch they vanished into air.

The streets became but dirt beneath their tread,
Returned to splendor after they had passed,
And when in some great hall their footsteps led,
The walls collapsed about the mortal caste.

And they were grieved that they could not attain
To all the glory of the heavenly reign.

XV

Test of the Man of Sin

A massive mansion stood above the rest,
And in the entrance stood the Man of Sin,
He passed the threshold with an empty jest,
And strange procedures did he find within.

He saw a mass of gems in glad array,
But when on some he lay his selfish hold,
They vanished in his hands, and dripped away,

Except a shining knife of flaming gold.
A punctured corpse revived his ancient laws,
And as he poised himself to do the deed,
The dagger melted from his rotten claws,

The corpse eluded him with ghostly speed.
And failing thus, himself he tried to kill,
But every muscle failed to do his will.

XVI

Test of the Man of Faith

He waited for awhile, as Faith arrived
To see such treasures as the structure held,
And on the happy one his envy thrived,

Against his soul his filthy heart rebelled.
Before Faith's sight appeared a brilliant world,
A Ruler spoke, and offered all he saw,
Before his eyes were crude delights unfurled,

But he refused with hesitating awe.
Within a luring cradle in his path,

A living form of beauty met his eyes,
But well he knew the snaring aftermath,

And all her pleading sin he did despise.
A crown was put before his startled view,
He shunned its earthly gold, and then withdrew.

XVII

Test of the Man of Hypocrisy

Hypocrisy approached the threshold fair,
And lost all pow'r to sense the Master's plot,
So when his gaze had met the mansion's glare,
He could not bear to leave the stuff to rot.

He chose the clearest jewels from the mass,
But as his fingers touched a brilliant stone,
It's brazen sparkling changed it into glass,
And all the walls resounded with his groan.

His eyes beheld a form with subtle grace,
She beckoned him, and offered of herself,
She promised youth, if he her path would trace,

So on he sped, to catch the fleeing elf
But passing through a door, he slipped and fell,
And found himself outside the citadel.

XVIII

Test of the Man of Discontent

As Discontent passed through the beauteous halls,
He, also, gazed upon the glory there,
He saw the works of God upon the walls,
And to it all he lent a sultry stare.

His eyes saw all but they could not transmit
Their message to his earthly hardened heart,
In Beauty he could see no benefit,

Nor could his soul discern the heavenly art.
He passed through every phase, and still his eyes
Were useless, for he failed to see the Lord,
Expecting more, his plight he did despise,

His soul with God was far from in accord.
And as he left the mansion's tow'ring gate,
His heart sank down, he realized his fate.

XIX

Test of the Man of Disappointment

At last came Disappointment to the manse,
And as he gazed upon the bright display,
A lurid dullness tempered every glance,
For he could see but dirt, and rotten clay.

His poisoned mind could not obey his sight,
Which scanned the beauteous glory of the place,
And not a thing arouse his soul's delight,
For he could not perceive the Master's grace.
The disappointed wretch expected more,
And thought that heaven did not hold enough,

For all the seeming clay he did deplore,
His powerless soul seemed now its own rebuff.
And as he left the mansion's emptiness,
He sighed for heaven's lack of loveliness.

XX

The Summons

A glowing fountain rose beside the road,
Inviting parching throats to quench their thirst,
And everyone who passed the water, showed
His eagerness to sip the fluid first.

The water seemed to have a living heart,
And as they tried to get a soothing drop,
Their lips touched fire, and nearly burned apart
The water spoke their anxiousness to stop:

Ye cannot long stop here, O men of earth!
But travel on to where your God will be,
And every soul the master finds is worth
Eternal life will surely drink of me.

So go, and seek the Judgment of the King
I am the Christ! Of life the living Spring!

XXI

The Great Judge

The God of all the world awaited them
In glory, far exceeding earthly charm,
Beneath what might have been a diadem?
His splendor shone, and caused a great alarm.

Their eyes could not discern His heav'nly face,
For in its stead they saw the dancing rays,
But all could feel the presence of His grace,
And toward His throne they lent their wond'ring gaze.

In majesty He beckoned to the mass,
His unseen force made everyone come near,
And o'er His threshold mortal man did pass,
With hopes that He would make the vision clear.
The just Creator called the slaves of strife,
And one by one they came in search of life.

XXII

Judgement of the Man of Sin

The Man of Sin approached the God of all,
With eyes so blurred he could not see his King.
Before the throne in answer to the call,
His vile and spotted soul he had to bring.

And thus God spoke, and pierced him with His glance:
Ah, all these places ye have just traversed
Are only tests to give me one last chance?

To separate the blessed ones from the cursed.
A little of your soul I gave in trust,
How shameful have you rendered it to me!
Ah, mortal sin, much lower than the dust,

Go purge your heart in yonder blood-rent sea!
From evil seeds an evil harvest springs,
So with what's left to you seek higher things.

XXIII

Judgment of the Man of Discontent

Reluctantly the Man of Discontent,
Appeared before the Judge of every sphere,
In sad obeisance by the throne he bent,
He felt his wretched life would cost him dear.

A calmness reigned supreme, as someone spake:
"You have not lived at all, O foolish one,
Your bit of soul from me you deigned to take,
And let it melt to naught, and now 'tis done.

I gave you happiness, which you refused,
You thought it not enough to grace your state;
I gave you moral gems, which you misused,
You spent them ill, and at too great a rate.

The talents you have spoiled are worthless dust,
You must be born again to gain My trust."

XXIV

Judgment of the Man of Disappointment

The Disappointed One approached the throne,
And to him, too, the Lord refused his sight,
While waiting there he felt he was alone,
Until a voice came through the seeming night:

"O slothful man, that cannot recognize
The beauty of the earthly gifts of God,
And when in heaven, continues to despise
The glory here, so far above Earth's sod,

You cannot see, because your sight is spoiled,
Your heart is twisted into hideous form,

The bit of soul I gave you clean is soiled
You failed to see the sunshine in the storm.

Redeemed you cannot be, so now depart,
Destroy the selfishness within your heart!"

XXV
Judgment of the Man of Hypocrisy

And then came blind Hypocrisy, to stand
Before the King, to answer for his life,
He felt convinced that in this Promised Land
He'd long remain, escaping victory's strife.
But soon he shuddered, as he heard the voice:

"Thou man of earthly thoughts, and double ways,
Who for the right hast failed to make the choice,
You cannot have the Master's heavenly praise.
Your mortal skin is torn from off your heart,

And bares before the light your rotten soul,
Distorted, black and low in every part,

So poor a prize to render at the goal!
The lives that you have lived condemn you here,
So go, and keep the part that's left you clear.

XXVI
Judgement of the Man of Faith

A stillness reigned, and all about the throne,
A vivid light poured down its whitish rays,
The sad, depressive air of sin had flown,
As on the Man of Faith the Master's gaze

Had fallen, while his eyes beheld the King:
"Thou seeker of the Right, your life has been
The glory of My Faith, and you shall bring
To those who failed, a cleanser for their sin.

I praise you, for I know your smallest thought,
That you have tried to live the way I meant,
And life to come will be with beauty fraught,
For you dispersed the glory that I sent.

The earth is much embellished by your life,
As you emerge a victor from the strife!"

The Ballad of Jim DeFoe

I

'Twas back in '96 or so, we sailed from 'Frisco Bay
Along with us was Jim DeFoe, a merry one, and
    gay.
We headed for the Orient, and left each one his
    home,
For now our gallant ship was sent across the luring
    foam.
From dawn till dark we looked to Jim to make each
    day seem bright;
We always could rely on him to keep our spirits
    light.
For many days we sailed the sea, it seemed a half a
    year
Then land arose upon our lee, our journeys end was
    near!

II

We thought we'd struck the Malay coast, and we
    prepared to land,
But that which puzzled us the most was why this
    silent strand
Should be the place our skipper meant to cast our
    anchor in,
This place could hardly represent the port we hoped
    to win,
As night came on we went below, and gathered in
    the hold,
All eyes were centered on DeFoe, all listened as he
    told
The story of a South Sea isle, which he had once
    explored,
And then at length he stopped awhile his fancy
    higher soared.

III

Then suddenly he stared at us; his face was all
    aflame,
With eyes of fire he glared at us, and called out two
    by name.
He asked them if they'd go with him, ashore this
    lonely night,
Although the sky was growing dim, and stars sank
    out of sight.
They first began to hesitate, but soon they joined
    DeFoe,
 And though the hour was getting late, they left the
    rest below.
I went above to see them leave, and watched them
    fade from sight,
My blinking eyes could scarce believe that Jimmy's
    mind was right.

IV

And when an hour had hardly passed, the sky burst
    forth in storm,
The wind increased and bent our mast, and it was
    none too warm.
And through it all we thought of Jim, the folly of
    his act,
We thought of those who went with him, it did not
    seem a fact.
When morning came the storm was o'er, the sun
    began to glow,
But not a sign was seen on shore, of reckless Jim
    DeFoe.
And then we told the skipper all that passed the
    night before,
How Jimmy left before the squall, and headed for
    the shore.

V

The old man sent a party out to find the missing
    three;
We searched the country round about, but ne'er a
    soul did see.
 But just as we had lost all hope, we saw a fire
    ahead,

And at the bottom of the slope, we stopped as if
    struck dead.
A group of natives had appeared, and gathered in a
    ring,
So to their fire our course we steered, prepared for
    anything.
The crowd we covered with our guns, while some
    one searched the hut,
We could not find the missing ones, so their
    acquaintance cut.

VI

But as we left I saw a grin beneath one's shaggy
    hair,
I wondered what was ailing him, and followed close
    his stare
I saw a pot above the flame, which hid a savory
    dish,
And then I saw their artful game, that pot
    contained no fish!
I felt a shudder as I saw, in cold reality,
That from that hungry isle we'd draw no
    hospitality.
But all my life I'll always see, wherever I may go,
The pot that held the foolish three, among them
    Jim DeFoe!

To West Point

On the Eve of the Army-Navy Game, 1923
(Score: Army 0, Navy 0, in the mud, at the Polo Grounds)

We've flung defiance to your ears,
With little love for you,
And many skies have heard our cheers
For our own chosen few.

In seeming hatred while we stood,
And viewed the Grey-clad hosts
Rush on the field, we scarcely could
Suppress our thwarted boasts.
For in our hearts we've cherished none
But those in brilliant blue,
Indignant at the kindly sun
That also shines on you.

II

The bitter feeling of a day,
In dominating force,
Has glorified our own array,
And justified our course.
But as the sunsets stately glow
Subdues the noonday heat,

We soon forget the grievous foe,
And cast away conceit.
The leaven works upon our hearts,
Which are as weak as yours,
And flimsy hatred soon departs,
We even up the scores.

III

Our petty struggles fade away,
They're only playful strife,
Our bitterness is laid away,
This not a part of life;
We'll not begrudge the merit due
To men as good as we,

While all their prejudice subdue,
In friendly loyalty.
And as we stand in friendship's glow,
And drink to days of old,
We'll pledge to Benny Havens O,
To black, and grey, and gold!

The Port Condenser

Dedicated to a worn out main condenser of the
USS Florida in 1923

The night belonged to poets' dreams,
As we traversed old Neptune's realm
Then from the sullen silence came
A thunderbolt that jarred the helm
The bulkheads aft had fallen through,
As someone woke the engineer,
And when at last he reached the scene,
He told us all to have no fear,
'Twas just the port condenser.

We were steaming rather easy,
Bound for pleasant foreign shores,
While I hugged the double bottoms,
Rather than perform my chores.
In the night a roaring tide-riff
Rushed upon me, while I swam,
Through the water, salt and bitter,
To surmount the broken dam,
That ancient port condenser.

The years have come, the same years gone,
While I've been faithful to the sea,
I've met life bravely, death with fear,
And lived through deeds less good than free.
But happiness is not complete,
My heart is still weighed down with woe,
And I will never die until
The engineer shall go below,
And fix that port condenser!

The Ring

Upon receiving Class Ring
United States Naval Academy 1925

I

The potter took a formless mass of clay,
And strove to change it to a thing of shape,
But after it appeared to be complete,
Displeased, he did not cease to touch and scrape.

II

At last, the finished vase in beauty robed,
Was placed in view its beauty to display,
But mishap caused the thing to fall and break,
It changed back to a mass of dust and clay.

III

We, too, are being formed from worthless clay,
And on the harder road we've just begun.
The hour is near when we shall have a ring,
In token of success already won.

IV

Let not that ring become the final goal,
But let it be an urge to higher things,
Nor let the work we've done decay and rot,
For then the band of gold no glory brings.

V

Ambition dawned within our souls,
Then effort, zeal, and work did bring
Reward for all that's gone before,
The symbol of it all . . . the ring.

Sob of a Seagoing Bachelor

I

The restless lure of the ocean, and the life that one
lives there,
Has a greater place within us, than your lips and
flowing hair.
We bachelors find happiness on yonder foaming
brine,
Without the worries of those who fell for the
marriage line.
And sailing the rolling billows, with their taste of
salty spray,
We live the life of a sailor, nor envy the common
lay.

II

Hail to the glorious waters, with their call we can't
resist,
While we leave our homes and sweethearts,
for the realms of vigorous mist.
But although we linger awhile, far out on the angry
foam,
We are satisfied with our mothers,
and the place that they call home.
We do not dread to be married, and be true to only
one,
But 'tis better to love unmarried,
with a pledge of our hearts to none.

III

So my darling and loving sweethearts,
   with your lures so spicy and fair,
Though we take your love and caresses,
   we know how little you care.
We sympathize with your plight,
   with your hollow and short-lived love,
While others bathe in your glances,
   for whom you are turtledove.
But we'll never refuse your kisses, for we're off to
   sea very soon,
To leave you to others more trusting than us, the
   sea, and the moon!

Donald O. Burling and Dodie Frost

Look to the Mirror

Dost thou think the day is dreary,
And thy work so hard and weary;
Dost thou find much trouble,
With thy cares all double,
Look to the mirror for thine answer
For there thou wilt find the cause of it.

Dost thy friend find life so pleasant,
With each crow-like task a pheasant;
Are his burdens lighter
And his skyline whiter
Look the mirror for thine answer
But wait! Thou wilt see but thine own plight.

The Battle

I

The innocent and unsuspecting air
Lay peaceful in her charming earthly lair;
The lazy sunlight's penetrating glare
Soon flushed the noonday's cheeks with crimson rare;
The flowered fields dozed on, without a care,
Of danger's sword their souls were not aware,
For peace and calm was reigning everywhere,
With not a sign to mar the firmament.

II

But suddenly upon the ear did flare
The drummer's flourish and the bugler's blare,
The cannon roared, their victims to ensnare;
The field was rent in twain, *beyond repair,*
And blood flowed free, with plenty more to spare,
While vassals' swords prolonged the dread despair,
The strife continued in its ravishment,
Until it waned for lack of nourishment.

III

As twilight came, the carnal festival
Had no one left to share its funeral?
And peace returned to claim its pedestal;
The sad-eyed stars, with gaze so lyrical,
Perused the quiet calm, the prodigal,
Returned to mend the ruined interval
The flowers bloomed in beauty magical,
Their blush made red by streams unnatural.

IV

The dawn arose in silent majesty,
Upon an earth that slept in travesty,
And shed a little glory on its face,
As if to pierce its shallow modesty.
In mortal sleep was lost its greediness,
Which slept beside its earthly foolishness,
 In broad command of all the wilderness,
While in the East in firmamental grace,
The sun awoke with shining hopefulness.

V

And Life bestirred itself, and saw the day,
And plunged headstrong into the mass of clay,
In eagerness, to rise amid the fray,
And seize the spoils that lavished this domain.
But enemies seemed armed with cruel hate,
And, delving in their stores inadequate,
Life, being tired, emerged to abdicate
The field that promised nothing but disdain.

VI

Refreshing dusk relieved the day's ill heat,
And cooled the fountain's burning rivulet,
For now the weary sun could not compete
With stars that graced their lofty minaret.
The peaceful earth in tiredness went to rest
Beneath the calmness of the languid night,
And Life, relinquishing its plunging quest.
Ascended from its stormy, earthly plight,
And gliding down the smooth and phantom stream,
Rejoiced upon the ending of the dream.

The New Spring Poem

Ah, Spring is here again, my friend,
The snow is on the ground
The birds are warbling last year's songs,
The sun cannot be found.
The leaves are creeping on the trees
They crackle with the gale
The brook lags slowly to the sea
 Beneath its icy veil.

As far as you can see from here
Is clothed in verdure green,
The grass? The ground? The leaves? The trees?
The parlor rug, I mean.
You think me bugs to write this stuff
This poem to expound?
Ah, Spring is here again, my friend,
The snow is on the ground!

Dawn on Lexington Common

On April nineteenth, seventy five,
Our Captain Parker stood alive
In front of Pitcairn's redcoats straight,
To scrve as Adams' tempting bait.

The pawns of freedom's gamble trod
Out on the Common with their God,
Not knowing how each silent gun
Would send the British on the run.

The major tried to skip the trap,
And thus evade the pois'nois rap,
But hotheads 'mong the raw young bucks,
Could not resist the sitting ducks

A flash up there, a pistol here,
A few more random shots rang clear
And then a futile answ'ring shot
A cold war suddenly came hot.

The trap slammed shut, and poor King George,
With eight dad men his chains did forge
Pandora's box did not emit
In any mighty roaring fit,
Just oozing out so innocent
With such a tiny incident
A powder flash on Parker's ridge
Had lit a shot at Concord's bridge.

While Hancock toasted Adams' wit
In luring Gage into the pit,
And Smith and Pitcairn played their part
On treach'rous seas without a chart,

Those kings themselves became but pawns
In God's own plans for better dawns,
And brothers joined the bloody role
To gain the unknown common goal.

The fame is not for Lexington,
Where nothing but confusion won,
Nor Concord's bridge deserves the praise
Those pseudo patriots' voices raise.

Nor battles lost, nor battles won,
Nor any duties left undone
Could change the course of God's decree
That man should strive for liberty.

In human frailties all abound,
But God's command's a clarion sound
Some shot, somewhere will always bring
The message from our only King.

Dawes Also Rode

The glory bells all peal the toll
    For rider Paul Revere,
But how he failed the further goal
    Those bells do not make clear.

'Tis true romance did cloak his trip,
    With petticoat so fair,
To dull his oarlocks' noisy grip
    En route to Charlestown Square.

'Tis true he got to Medford town,
    And wakened Captain Hall,
And then from there proceeded down
    The road to waken all.

He reached the town of Lexington,
    To bring the hopeful cue,
That Adams' patient ruse had won
    What arms could never do?

Our Adams planned to trick King George
    To let his brothers' blood,
And with it feed the fiery forge
    In freedom's massive flood.

The job was only partly done
    When Paul rode into town,
For much was needed ere the sun
    Should raise its bristling frown.

A half hour after Paul's short lope,
    The vet'ran Dawes arrived,
Our William covered greater scope
    Than Paul Revere contrived.

No colorful romance in him,
    To capture poet's whim,
Just cold and calculated nerve,
    With which to gladly serve

In freedom's cause, along with those
   Within whose hearts there rose
The cry for independence from
   A yoke so cumbersome.

He knew the job, and every trick,
   To outwit redcoat foe,
In every opening so quick
   To add to British woe.

As farmer, miller, vagabond,
   He mixed with foreign friends,
With casual ease he got beyond
   The British outer ends.

With bag of meal astride his horse,
   The simple miller rode
As salesman, on the longer course
   To wake each dark abode.

From Lexington they both began
   The trip to concord's green,
Alerting every minuteman
   That redcoats had been seen.

A Doctor Prescott met our crew
   A short way from the start,
He knew the road, and offered to
   Contribute his small part

Along the way two men arose,
   Revere called out to them
Then two more, all in British clothes,
   Disturbed the stratagem

Assigned our riders of the night.
   Revere was easy prey
But Dawes and Prescott reeled in flight,
   To keep alive the fray.

The unassuming Prescott went
    To all on Concord's road,
While Dawes lured redcoats off the scent
    From rebel powder stowed

Within the town that Smith had planned
    To strip of shot and shell.
The warning gave the patriot band
    The time to drain the well.

Revere deserves the great acclaim
    That sounds from freedom's bells
In things of brass a worthy name
    And Hist'ry loudly tells

The story of the famous ride.
    To where the ending, pray?
In Lincoln's woods he did collide
    With redcoats in his way.

Unhorsed so rudely by the foe,
    Our hero plodded back
Beneath the moonlight's lonely glow,
    To find the welcome shack

In Lexington, whence all began
    The trek to Concord town.
The one had failed, but two outran
    The bar to fame's renown.

So sound the bells for Paul Revere,
    Who shared with William Dawes?
The rides of men that midnight clear,
    Who rode in freedom's cause?

But don't forget Dawes' greater ride,
    Nor Prescott's priceless jaunt,
They, too, performed on freedom's side,
    Against the Briton's taunt.

No single ride, no single man,
    Deserves exclusive praise
It takes the hearts of all to fan
    The flames of God's own blaze.

Part IV

Music of Burling and Frost

Lyrics by Donald Burling, recorded by Dodie Frost

O Wondrous Love

1976

O wondrous love of God divine,
Flee into this heart of mine,
And I will let it freely flow
To every creature that I know.
Let Thy love rain freely down,
And I'll not ask Thee for a crown.
Just love and service for my God
Is all the path that need be trod

Chorus

> *This is my song of love for thee*
> *This is my earnest plea*
> *O teach me how to serve and love*
> *The same as Thee above*
> *The same as Thee, O God divine,*
> *And flee into this heart of mine*

O show me just enough to know
The way that Thou would have me go
And with Thy love to light my heart,
I'll never stray from Thee apart
This is my prayer to Thee complete
That we in love shall always meet
And work in service to all men
Until Thou call me home again.

Chorus

O come into my soul, dear God
And lead me in the path Thou trod
O let me linger by Thy side
And in Thy love may I abide
O guide me down the rocky road
And help me carry all my load
That Thou assign to me to bear
And I will carry all my share

Chorus

This is my song of love for Thee
This is my earnest plea
O teach me how to serve and love,
The same as Thee above
The same as Thee, O God divine
And flee into this heart of mine.

Holy Spirit

Holy Spirit, like a river, flow into my heart anew,
At Thy feet may I deliver Glory, praise and love for
  You.
Holy Spirit, hold me ever, In Thine arms when I am
  weak.
By my side please walk forever, While Thy will I
  always seek.
Holy Spirit, take me to Thee, Keep me for Thy very
  own,
And I pray You always guide me, To the fields that
  must be sown.

Holy Spirit, like the thunder, Come down to this
  soul of mine,
Let me rally at the wonder of my love and help
  divine,
Holy Spirit, let me tarry Always by Thy loving side,
All the load Thou bidst me carry, I shall by Thy
  will abide
Holy Spirit, keep on flowing into me, Thy humble
  one,
All the while I keep on knowing. That Thy will is
  always done.

Holy Spirit, how I need You, Never leave me all
  alone,
I will always try to heed You, while You keep me
  for Thine own.
Holy Spirit, lift the flood gate, Pour Your love into
  my heart,
While my flight to you must first wait, Till I finish
  all my part.
Holy Spirit, how I love you, How I glory in Thy
  Power,
Glory, Honor, praises of You, Serve me in my ev'ry
  hour.

Flowing Spirit

Spirit flowing through my soul,
Be my comfort and my guide
Show me to Thy chosen goal
Always linger by my side
How I feel Thy presence dear
How I love to hear Thy voice
Then I know You're always near
How it makes my heart rejoice.

Spirit flowing through my heart,
Filling it with all Thy love
Never shall your child depart
From my God who reigns above
Even tears and sadness fade
When You put Your hand in mine
For Your work I'm surely made
With Your help that is divine

Spirit flowing in my tears
Even mighty Jesus cried
Stay with me through all the years
While I in Thine arms abide
Spirit flowing through my soul
Spirit flowing through my heart
In Thy way Thou make me whole
Loving Lord Thou surely art.

In the Valley

I prayed to reach the highest peak
From which to lead a mighty horde
And fame of greatness I would seek
To turn my people to the Lord
I prayed to have the greatest task
To win all people back to God
To lead His army I would ask
Along the Glory Road to trod

Chorus

> *Our God is in the darkest valley*
> *With those who need His help and love*
> *And with His workers there I'll rally*
> *Until He takes me home above*

I prayed the greater work to do
Than all the little jobs I got
The work is great, the workers few
My talents could do such a lot
But every time I sought the top
God kept me in the vales below
He needed Workers for the crop
To make the harvest brighter glow.

Chorus

So now I never ask to see
The sunshine on the mountain top
Just let me in the valley be
Where work for You will never stop
I'll be content to stay below
While others seek the Glory Road
Your valley love will always glow
More bright than in the high abode.

Chorus

The Greatest Love

Spirit of Faith, weakest of all
Come to my heart, build me a wall
Close to my Lord, held in his fold
Help me to trust, while You doth hold
All my heart, close to Your side,
Where I shall stay, long to abide

Chorus

> *Oh Faith that will not fail my heart*
> *Oh hope that never will depart*
> *And Love, the greatest gift of all,*
> *Forever will I heed Your call*

Spirit of Hope, precious to life,
Hold me so close, strong through the strife
When shadows fall, only doth Hope
Hold up my heart, far down the slope
Keep the spark live, shiny and bright
Straight to Your fold, heavenly Light

Chorus

Spirit of Love, greatest of all
Hold me, dear God, don't let me fall
Give me the Faith closer to Thee
Give me the Hope, glory to see
Give me Your love, gracious and deep
Always with You, never to weep

Chorus

I'll Take You Home

I'll take you to your home, my child,
When all your work is done below
Across the oceans wide and wild
To where your Father's light doth glow
Your faith has kept your love alive
I've watched you grow in works and deeds,
So when you finally arrive
Your God will furnish all your needs.

Chorus

> *Oh, I will take you home, dear one*
> *To where your heart is filled with love*
> *Where there will be no setting sun*
> *And glory reigns with God above*

I'll take you to your glory home
To where your new work just begins
No storms to rage or sees to roam
Away from earth's beguiling sins
Your hope will shine in heaven's light
Your steps I watch so you don't fall
Your God will be a holy sight
When comes the day that He doth call

Chorus

I'll take you home to peace and rest
To where you live beside your God
And lay your head on His warm breast
No rocky roads on earth to trod
Your love will live beside your Lord
Your hope will flourish in the light
And God will take you safe on board
Oh, what a glorious, heav'nly sight.

Chorus

**The next ten songs were recorded by Dodie Frost
in Nashville.**

Slow Boat to Heaven

There's a boat that sails each day
Past my door, it's on its way.
I got my ticket for the trip to heaven.
What a lovely ride to the home where I belong.
I can hear the angel's song.
I'm waiting for that slow boat to heaven.

Ev'ry day it sails on through
On a sea of skies so blue.
Ev'ry trip it makes will bring me closer to my Lord.
Ev'ry day I work for God,
Walking where His steps have trod.
When he calls me I'll be ready to get on board.

Now it's time to sail away,
On a bright and happy day,
Sail toward that home that's waiting on the other side.
Little boat please carry me, 'cross the wild and stormy sea.
For I know your Captain, my Lord, will be my guide.

Slow Boat To Heaven

Donald Burling

Beegie Adair

Donald O. Burling and Dodie Frost

I Will Be True

In all my life I will be true
No matter how You lead me, Lord
Though darkest night to morning dew,
I'll meet with You in sweet accord.

No fame or fortune do I seek,
For Love and service will suffice.
Though darkness sometimes leaves me weak,
I'll cling to Thee and never ask the price.

> *No matter what my fate may be,*
> *I'll always cling so close to Thee*
> *I will be true, dear Lord divine,*
> *I will be true, forever Thine*

He loves and cares and heals my pain.
He shields my heart and guards my soul
For Him I'll do what He ordains
And try to reach His Holy goal.

When days are dark I'll cling to Him
And do His work the best I can.
When days are bright I'll sing to Him
And give my all to live His master plan.

> *No matter what my fate may be,*
> *I'll always cling so close to Thee*
> *I will be true, dear Lord divine,*
> *I will be true, forever, Thine.*

I Will Be True

Donald Burling

Beegie Adair

I Hear Jesus Calling

I hear Jesus calling with a message true.
He says stop your stalling, live your life anew.
I hear angels singing, bells are ringing.
Jesus is calling out to me and you.

Listen well, my brother, to His message clear
God is watching over you, he is always near
Listen well, my sister, can you heed the call.
God is watching over all.

I hear Jesus calling with a message true.
He says stop your stalling, live your life anew
I hear angels singing, bells are ringing.
Jesus is calling out to me and you.

Listen to His preaching, shouting out the way.
He can help you find the path to a brighter day.
You have all His caring. He needs all your love.
God is watching from above.

I Hear Jesus Calling

Donald Burling

Beegie Adair

Leave Your Sorrow

Leave your sorrow, count your blessings,
For your God is ever with you still
All your sadness put behind you
Try to do your loving Father's will

Leave your sorrow, God is with you
Spread a smile and dry up all your tears
Ever present, God will find you
He's been there through all the lonely years.

Leave your sorrow, God is with you
If you take His willing, loving hand.
Sadness passes. Love will greet you.
Turn your eyes 'tward the nearby promised land.

Leave your sorrow, count your blessings,
For your God is ever with you still
All your sadness put behind you
Try to do your loving Father's will.

Leave Your Sorrow

Donald Burling   Beegie Adair

Swing Down Sweet Lord

Swing low sweet chariot,
comin' for to carry me home.
Swing down to my waiting place,
Chariot of my precious Lord.

Swing down when I finish life's great race,
I would like to get on board.
When I finish all my earthly chores.
And I'm tired and long for Thee,
Sweet and precious are Thy heav'nly shores.
Waiting there to welcome me.

Swing down when I finish life's great race,
I would like to get on board.
When You bring me to that heav'nly shore,
That I've seen from Earth below,
Free from sadness I will dwell with Thee,
Living in that heavn'ly glow.

Swing Down to my waiting place,
Chariot of my precious Lord.
Swing down when I finish life's great race,
I would like to get on board.

Swing Down Sweet Lord

Donald Burling

Beegie Adair

Jesus is My Sunshine

Jesus is my sunshine, shining over the hill.
Jesus is my lifeline,
Molding my will.
Jesus is my starlight, guiding my way,
Walking in daylight hand in hand through ev'ry day.
Jesus is my sunshine, pouring out His blessings.
His love is all mine, and He makes it right.
Jesus walks beside me.
He will always guide me
Through the darkness and through the light
Jesus is my sunshine, watching ev'ry hour
He will be my guideline I will do His will.
Jesus help me and hold me
Let your arms enfold me
Up the long and lonely hill.
Jesus is my sunshine, shining over the hill
Jesus is my lifeline molding my will.
Jesus is my starlight guiding my way,
Walking in daylight hand in hand through ev'ry day.

Jesus Is My Sunshine

Donald O. Burling and Dodie Frost

Beautiful Lord

Beautiful Lord, bountiful Lord, stop at my heart,
 I pray.
Beautiful Lord, share with me all Thy love.
 Wash all my sins away.
Show me the road that I must trod,
 straight as the flight of the dove.
I am your servant for life, Oh God.
 Bless me with all Your love.
Walk with me always and show me the way.
 Teach me to follow Thy lead.
Heavenly Father, be with me each day.
 Give me the peace I need.
Beautiful Lord, bountiful Lord, stop at my heart,
 I pray.
Beautiful Lord share with me all Thy love.
 Wash all my sins away.

Beautiful Lord

Happy is the Lamb

I was lost but now I'm found, just a sheep that
went astray.
In the rocky, thorny ground, God did not find me
far away
In His heart I take my rest, Nourished by His
loving care.
Through His Grace His home I share.

Chorus

*Happy is the lamb He found. Happy is the soul He
saved.*
*Now I graze on hallowed ground, with His grace its
path is paved.*
Happy is the lamb he saved.

All His sheep will answer Him, ev'ry lamb that
went afar.
He will search all the mountains and the valleys
where you are.
If you answer to His call, He will answer back to
you
And your life will start anew.

Chorus

Now I'm happy with my god, now I always work
for Him.
No more rocky roads to trod, Just His lights that
never dim.
Come and join the happy throng, all His sheep are
in the fold.
Jesus' love is more than gold.

Chorus

Happy Is The Lamb

Donald Burling

Beegie Adair

1. I was lost but now I'm found, just a sheep that went a - stray. In the
2. All His sheep will an - swer Him, ev' - ry lamb that went a - far. He will
3. Now I'm hap - py with my God, now I al - ways work for Him. No more

rock - y, thorn - y ground, God did find me far a - way. In His heart I take my
search all the moun - tains and the val - leys where you are. If you an - swer to His
rock - y roads to trod, just His lights that ne - ver dim. Come and join the hap - py

rest, nour-ished by His lov - ing care. Through His Grace His home I
call, He will an - swer back to you. And your life will start a -
throng, all His sheep are in the fold. Je - sus' love is more than

share. Hap - py is the lamb He found.
new.
gold. Hap - py is the soul He saved. Now I

graze on hal-lowed ground, with His grace its path is— paved. Hap - py is the

lamb He saved.

I Praise Thee Lord

In the depths of the valley the path was so dark
  while I searched for a light to show me the way.
Then you walk'd by my side and You gave me
  strength to move toward a beautiful day.

Now I praise Thee, Lord, with my heart and my mind
  for Thy love and Thy guidance through the night
From the valleys so deep You lifted up my soul.
  I will walk in Your love and Your light.

Now the time is near when my work will be done
  and I'll walk by Your side in heaven above.
To my Lord, my God, I will always be true
  as I stand in the light of Your love.

Now I praise Thee, Lord, with my heart and my mind
  for Thy love and Thy guidance through the night
From the valleys so deep You lifted up my soul.
  I will walk in Your love and Your light.

I Praise Thee Lord

Donald Burling

Beegie Adair

Slowly

In the depths of the val - ley the path was so dark while I
time is near when my work will be done and I'll

searched for a light to show me the way. Then You walk'd by my
walk by Your side in heav - en a - bove. To my Lord, my

side and You gave me strength to move t'ward a beau - ti - ful
God, I will always be true as I stand in the light of Your

day. Now I praise Thee, Lord, with my heart and my
love.

mind for Thy love and Thy guid - ance through the night. From the

val - leys so deep You lift - ed up my soul. I will walk in Your

love and Your light. Now the walk in Your

love and Your light.

Closer to Thee

Closer to Thee, closer to Thee,
Oh let me be much closer to Thee.
Hear me, Oh Lord, Consider my plea.
You are my love, You are my heart.
You are my life, Lord, my life, Lord.
You are the god of my heart.

Love me, Oh Lord. Stand where I stand.
Walk with me, Lord, hold fast to my hand.
Lead me, Oh god, to the promised land.
You are my love, You are my heart.
You are my life, Lord, my life, Lord
You are the God of my heart.

Nearer to Thee, nearer to Thee.
Love me, Oh Lord, And make my heart free.
Stay with me, Lord, my comforter be.
You are my love, You are my heart.
You are my life, Lord, my life, Lord.
You are the God of my heart.

Closer To Thee

Donald Burling

Beegie Adair

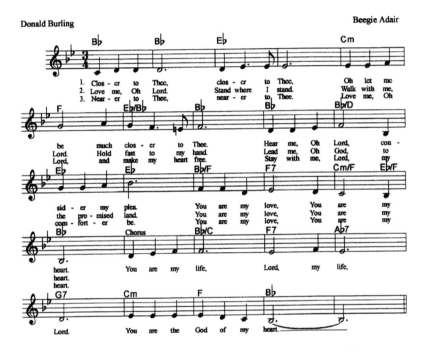

Part V

Selected Correspondence Through the Years

Editor's note: The art of letter writing is fast disappearing as short electronic notes and telephone calls replace traditional leisurely handwritten communication. Dodie Frost, the singer, and Donald Burling, the songwriter and his wife, Jennie, have written hundreds of letters to each other through the years. Although they had not met at the time of this book's writing, they shared their love of music and of the Lord as their friendship developed.
Some excerpts from Dodie and Donald's correspondence are included here for the information and insight they provide.

Penn Yan, N.Y.

February 12, 1990

Dear Dodie:

We were very happy to hear from you, but sad to hear of your family problems. . . I can empathize with you, since I had to go through twenty-two years of constant conflict with my first wife. I had to make some very tough decisions . . . since then, forty-two years with Jennie set me on a more normal and saner course . . .

Thanks a lot for the tapes. They are lovely. I am no longer active in music anymore. Too old and too tired have closed doors. I tried the Billboard contest last year but did not win. Of course, with tens of thousands of entries the odds were too terrific. Also thanks for the offer of the lead sheets, but I doubt that I have the stamina to tackle another try at it.

I have enclosed five songs that might interest you. They are among the best I ever wrote, and four of them have some excellent tunes composed by Tom Yanok (remember him?). You are free, with my full permission to use any of my stuff with no strings attached. If you like the tunes and the messages you might want to make tapes of them. If you do, I would sure love to have two or three. I might get our church choir to use them. If you can market them, they are all yours. Actually, all of my songs and music are yours for the asking. I am eighty-eight now. And can see nothing I can do at this late date, and if any of it might be useful to you, just charge it to memories of earlier years, when you contributed so much of your time and services on much of it. . . .

What makes you look so young in the band picture? It is wonderful that you have held them together so long. Keep it up. If you ever have the time and inclination to make a trip out here in the Finger Lakes region, the latchkey is out for you, anytime.

Lots of love to you and the children, Jennie and Don

Donald O. Burling and Dodie Frost

July 15, 1991

Dear Dodie:

We were so very happy to hear from you, Dodie. It has been
such a long time. . . At 90 you tend to slow down a little bit.
Jennie keeps busy in the garden and in the house, plus little
jobs for the church. We have a reasonable quota of old-age
problems, but are lucky to navigate much better than lots of
people in similar age groups. We walk, drive, take care of
ourselves, and perform regular chores (except hard work).
We can perform in areas where most old people have
discontinued action.

You have hit on a very nice idea for the album. I do think
you should cut the price to four dollars postpaid. I do not
need the tax deduction, as we no longer itemize. I have
plenty of albums if needed.

I think we have both had very interesting lives. I have
always tried everything that came my way. Some success
and lots of failures. But I would much rather try and lose
than cop out and not try at all. I have lived that way, and
have never regretted it . . . please concentrate on the present
and the future. That is all every one of us has left. Our
prayers go with you, and our love,

Always remembering you, Don and Jennie.

May 21, 1993

Dear Dodie:

. . . . It was wonderful to learn that you are around yet and getting your life rounded out the way that you want. . . .We remember and cherish the past, but do not try to substitute it as a way of life. Even my fantasies are not of the past. . . .

I feel as close to you as you do to me. I have always tried to help others that I come in contact with and who touch my soul and make me feel that they need help, even as I needed help—lots of it, in the past, back to my being 16 and alone in the world. I lived in a newsboy's lodging house in the bowery in Manhattan and worked in a factory during the War (World War I).

God sent me help, but I had to ride the freight trains to get to it (without my knowledge of course). I landed in Chicago broke, ended up in a Catholic shelter, and the priest got me into the Navy under age. At Great Lakes Training Station God sent me a buddy. To make a long story short, he took me to his home in Southern Illinois and his mother took, me in. My buddy got me to put in for a Navy prep school to try for appointment to the Naval Academy. My buddy died of pneumonia during the terrible winter of 1919–1920, and I went into the Academy alone and graduated.

His father and mother took me for their own and his mother is the one person I still love more than anyone I have ever known. Jennie knows this and accepts it. I have always tried to help others who need me to this day, even at my age. God has led me in this way of life and I love it. No wealth, no power, no luxuries. Just simple kindness and love. . . .

I have two studio tapes that you made at Baker Street Studios. Particularly, they contain what I judge as my three very best hymns. Do you want them? They include "Great Is His Love," "O Wondrous Love," and "I'll Take You

Home"—my best.

The new owners of the studio called me when they took over and called me and asked me if I wanted them. I only had to pay the postage. If you do not have Yanok's music sheets, I have them and will send copies if you want them.

We both love you very much. I pray for you every day, even while I did not know if your were living or not. Keep your course steady and don't be afraid to live and tackle every job that God gives you. He is sure one wonderful Operator.

Lots of love, Jennie and Don

May 24, 1994

Dear Dodie,

. . . It is wonderful that you keep our songs alive so well, Perhaps I am one of the writers whose works succeed after they are gone. That's OK with me. I do my duty by writing the songs. You are one of those angels who make them keep on living.

It is sure great to hear about your finally finding the happy road in working and enjoying the practice of your great talents. Finding that road at this time in your life is bound to be far more rewarding than finding it early and then losing it. . . .

Xmas 1994

Dear Dodie,

Every year you seem to be busier and busier but happier and happier. It is nice to see these older years turn out to be better than ever. Just think how awful it would be to reverse the order.

It is wonderful for you to plug my hymns. Perhaps it was meant for me not to see them succeed in my lifetime, but to grow after I am gone. That is much better than the reverse. Many good songwriters have had the same fate. I do not look for any fame, just for service. . . .

October, 6, 1995

Dear Dodie:

. . . Jennie has read the Bible through, cover to cover, eleven times during the past few years. During the eleventh trip through she recorded every single woman in the KJV who had a name, and wrote up a brief sketch of each one.

Some sketches were short because nothing extensive was recorded on them. Others varied a great deal in length. On many we had important information from other sources, especially from the Dead Sea Scrolls, recently discovered in the caves around Qumran at the head of the Dead Sea.

That was the area where the Essene Zealots lived, after their exile from Jerusalem in the last century B.C. That was Jesus's homeland, where he was born and raised and educated at the Essene Monastery and Seminary. I did the editing and arrangement, and had it printed locally. I was waiting for the printed copies to come out before answering. We just got them. Some copies are enclosed, together with my own booklet on the Crucifixion as described by class-mates and fellow alumnae at the seminary at Qumran, where Jesus graduated about 20 A.D. They were regular scribes, such as were trained and educated in Jewish history for at least 2,000 years, and recorded it in all of the scrolls of the Old Testament. You may not agree with the writings of Jesus's close friends and fellow alumnae, but I pass it along to you as information. I am not crusading. You make your own evaluations.

As for the promotion of our songs, we want you to negotiate as you please, and keep all of the proceeds as a reward for all of your input in our album activity. We are not rich, but we live comfortably, and do not need or desire any income from those songs. You have made them what they are, and deserve whatever you can get from them. . . .

With all of our love and hopes for you, Jennie and Don

P. S. We have 175 of our *Dodie Frost* albums left. Do you want them? If so, on one condition, they are for free.

October 13, 1995

Dear Dodie

Got your wonderful letter today. The picture looks great. We did not know if you would approve of my booklet. It undermines the fairy tale that modern Christian doctrine is built on. The modern doctrine is not what Jesus preached. He preached Judaism only, plus his ethics additives, and minus circumcision for Gentiles, for thirty years in the Roman Empire after Simon revived him. (Flushing out his stomach). Both booklets are going on sale in our local bookstore at the checkout counters. Two dollars for Jennie's and a dollar and fifty cents for mine. We only charge cost of printing. No profit. . . .

Herewith are thirty of Jennie's booklets and twenty of mine. Don't charge for them. Spread them out where they will do the most good. If there is any demand for them we'll get more printed. We will ship the records. There are one hundred and fifty of them left. One carton is partially full. Maybe I'll ship them UPS. This is a short note for now. I guess Christian Scientists are not as blind as most Christians. Jesus was greater as a human than as a God.

All our love, Jennie and Don

November 12, 1995

Dear Dodie:

Thank you very much for the beautiful flower arrangement that you sent me for my birthday. I am ninety-four and it is the first time that I have ever received a flower arrangement for my birthday. It was unexpected but very sweet of you. Hope you got the albums and the booklets okay. The two local bookstores are carrying the booklets.

I have enclosed three non-gospel songs that I wrote twenty-five years ago. They were so amateurish that I set them aside and went back to gospel songs, at which I am much better. In light of your revealing your North Carolina roots, I got a hunch to pass them along. They are all yours if you want them. Change them, rearrange them, or just throw them away. I like folk music as much as you do, but not so good at composing it.

Jennie is only eighty-six and in pretty good shape. Our doctor told me not to lift anything heavy (over five pounds) in front of Jennie. So I am doing very well. Jennie puts the trash out and does all the heavy work. I get off pretty easy, as long as I put on a new nitroglycerin patch every day to keep my main heart artery clear. I drive downtown sometimes. Jennie does most of the driving, but it really isn't too bad as long as we keep the few marbles in our brains that we were born with.

Lots of love to you on this best road that you are traveling now, Jennie and Don

May 26, 1996

Dear Dodie:

. . . We get our pleasure in walking with our God, and working for Him as best as our communication system with Him allows us to do.

It is wonderful how you are succeeding in getting our booklets distributed. It is better than we can do here. They are a mission with us, and not for profit for ourselves. They each cost about one dollar to print. If you have an opportunity to distribute them further, let us know how many copies of each that you will need and we will get them to you. I will get reprints if needed. We sent copies of Jennie's booklet to all forty ministers in our area, including Geneva. Only a few replied.

It is a shame that Jesus gets no credit at all for the thirty years of missionary work that he performed in the Roman Empire from 34 A.D. to 64 A.D. Paul and Peter did most of the legwork, together with their many aides, while Jesus spent most of his time at his headquarters in Rome, directing the campaigns. He had lots of help from the wealthy Herod family, most of who had been converted to Judaism by his grandfather Heli many years before. The Herod families stuck to Judaism through the years.

In 44 A.D. while Matthew was high priest in the Essene Zealot community at Qumran, he issued an edict declaring that all persons who were converted to Judaism by Jesus and his organization would be called "Christians." Today's Christians are a million miles away from that definition.

Paul and Peter were much younger than Jesus and could take the rough traveling all over the Empire, from Rome to Damascus, much better than Jesus. I know that Paul was fourteen years younger. He graduated from the Essene Zealot seminary at Qumran in 34 A.D. Jesus graduated in 20 A.D. Matthew, John the Baptist, Judas, and many other priests at Qumran were fellow alumni with Jesus.

Jesus' first child, a daughter named Tamar, was born in

September 33 A.D. She eventually married Paul in 53 A.D. in Cenchreae, a ritzy suburb outside of Corinth, where her father owned a house-church. Her name changed to Phoebe at her marriage. She is the one who was sent to Rome by Paul to deliver his letter to the Romans. Notice how much Paul praised his new wife in the first chapter of Romans. Incidentally, Mary Magdalene was Jesus's first wife. That's why she followed him at the cross, in the burial cave, and afterwards when he was rescued. All of my information comes from the Dead Sea Scrolls, written by priest scribes trained in the monasteries the same way as all scribes in Hebrew history. Many were fellow alumni with Jesus. . . .

Jennie has just gone through a tough siege with a near fatal intestine blockage in early January. She was saved just in time with major surgery. . . She is handling her problems with high courage, determination and prayer. But that is the story of her life. So it is just business as usual.

I have prostate cancer, discovered ten years ago when my prostate was removed. I also have an angina threat that is being warded off by wearing nitroglycerin patches for several years now. They keep the main heart artery loose and open. But I keep in shape. The new owners of the studio called me when they took over and called me and asked me if I wanted them. I only had to pay the postage. If you do not have Yanok's music sheets, I have them and will send copies if you want them. . . . Everything that we have done for you has been a pleasure. But it has been a two-way street. You have done a lot for us and are still working at it with our booklets. Our mutual relationship has been, and still is, a major blessing for all of us. . . .

Nov. 20, 1996

Dear Dodie:

. . . .The progress that you have made with our songs and albums has been marvelous, and makes us both very happy. You have the ability, the urge, and the opportunities for promoting and spreading them. We have tried but have no avenues or facilities for promoting them. Evidently God has chosen me to create them and He has chosen you to pick them up and carry them the rest of the way. I feel certain now that they will become very successful and helpful after I am gone, with you at the helm. That is very satisfying for me. I am ninety-five today and my life is nearly finished. I have always tried to operate to the fullest extent accordance with God's will and guidance. In spite of all of our failures neither one of us have any regrets. We have done our very best, and leave this life willingly with a clear conscience. . .

Jennie had major surgery in January for a blockage in her intestines. . . . Ovarian cancer had been inside of her for some time. It is the most difficult cancer to detect. Without the surgery for the intestines it would never have been detected, and she would have been gone by now. So you can see what an unusually radical method of communication God used to detect her cancer and get treatment started right away. Jennie has been having chemotherapy treatment every three weeks since February. . . .

I have enclosed a set of what I consider my seven best hymns. I know that you have some of them, but I wanted to make sure that you did not miss one or two of them.

You are in our regular daily prayers, and always will be. You are a real jewel in the crown of our lives.

With all of our love always, Jennie and Don

February 25, 1997

Dear Dodie

Enclosed are thirty copies of another booklet that I have written. The author of the book from which the excerpts are taken, Dr. Barbara Thiering, who also wrote *Jesus and the Riddle of the Dead Sea Scrolls,* has translated the entire *Book* of Revelation, verse by verse, from the Pesher imagery and visions into plain English.

It is amazing how those writers encoded the story of the history of the Judaic Christian movement in the first century into such terms as calf, lion, beast, fig tree, lamb, Moon, Sun, Satan, no one, thunder, lightening, and hundreds of other words and terms, into representing real people, real things, and real events. But this woman has done it, and has become one of the two best Biblical scholars in the world. The other expert is a French Catholic priest, Geza Vermes, but the pope will not allow him to publish anything about Hebrew history later than about 100 B.C. It would knock the Catholic Church for a loop.

Her recent book on Revelation, *Jesus of the Apocalypse,* was published in February of last year in Sydney and London. It is in the bookstores throughout England and Australia, and is a bestseller. She has not been able to get any printer or publisher to print it in the United States for two years. It does not violate any law or postal regulation, but the media and the modern Christian church have such powerful retaliatory capacity that no publisher so far has been brave enough to publish it.

I have a copy of the book. Some very dear friends of ours in London sent it to us for Christmas. It is loaded with the amazing history of the Judaic Christian movement in the first century. One amazing thing that I learned was that Matthew Annas ran the whole show in the entire Empire from Ephesus. He was the pope-priest of that area. Jesus worked under him as a sort of field commander and CEO, and Paul and Peter were—co-leaders doing most of the legwork. Remember, the Annas family (Matthew Annas, etc) were always very close to Jesus's family since the days of Jesus's grandfather, Jacob-Heli. Heli converted the Herod family to Judaism.

I have just mailed out one hundred and fifty copies of this booklet to all of the ministers in this area (Geneva and Elmira yellow pages). I am now waiting for the bombs to drop on our home. I have also enclosed your copyright form, signed. I am certainly very happy for the tremendous job that you have done with our albums. I don't expect anything too great to happen in my lifetime remaining, but do hope for your further success after I am gone. I think that it is amazing how much progress you have made already.

Jennie went off of chemotherapy in December. The cancer (ovarian cancer) has started back up a little. We do not know what the future holds. . . .

If you have use for more pamphlets, let me know. It is amazing how much 1 have learned in the last five years. I really wonder how I lasted the first ninety years, being as dumb as I used to be. But God has His own timetable, and decided to wait this long before doing a real big teaching job on me. I will always accept His timetable.

April 25, 1997

Dear Dodie,

Thanks for your last letter. It must be wonderful to get your family together so good at this time of your life. It is also wonderful to hear that you like my booklet. It is quite controversial with present day Christian beliefs, but the truth is far greater and stronger than the myth. It is tragic that Jesus was far greater in real life, from A.D. 34 to A.D. 70, with his son and grandson carrying on in his footsteps for many more years after that, and never gets one day's credit for those extra forty years. People could still believe that he was resurrected from the dead, and still give him credit for keeping on living.

I am enclosing two copies of my thesis on the entire Book of Revelation, as explained in Dr. Thiering's book, *Jesus of the Apocalypse*. The Book of Revelation has far more real history in it than the rest of the New Testament. All it needed was a translator, both of it and the Dead Sea Scrolls. Fortunately, Emperor Constantine and his brilliant staff of writers could not translate it when they radically revised the rest of the New Testament in the fourth century. Dr. Thiering can do just that.

I only made fifty copies, as I do not know how it might go over on a broad basis. The Four Horsemen is a popular story, and more attractive to the general public, though the truth may tread on a lot of important toes. If you know a few important people to have a copy, I can send you a few more copies. Brave preachers and honest Biblical scholars might enjoy it. Incidentally, a very close friend of ours in London was kind enough to send us a copy of Thiering's book. It is a bestseller in England and Australia, but banned by the Christian church hierarchy and the media in America. We have lost an awful lot of freedoms in the last fifty years.

Jennie is still getting better and better gradually. She has done remarkably well for her age and . . . of course, she is only eighty-seven years old, and seems to have quite a bit more time left.

I have worked on this thesis in these recent months. I may be able now to try to see what I can do about your suggested biography of me. I cannot do anything chronologically but maybe able to write down various phrases as they come up in my memory. They could be reshuffled chronologically later, as each item would be separate. I'll try, but it may take considerable time.

I sent out copies of my booklet on the Four Horsemen to one hundred forty-five ministers in this section of New York State, from Geneva down to Elmira and Corning. I have had only four replies, three good, one critical. My hope is that it will stir up a lot of preachers into doing a better job with their congregations, even though they do not contact me. . . .

We love you, Dodie, very much, Jennie and Don

July 12, 1997

Dear Dodie

It does not seem like two months has gone by since your last note. But the main purpose of calendars at our age is to keep track of doctors' appointments. We are happy that your move went along smoothly, and that you are very comfortable in your new quarters.

We recently got a survey questionnaire to fill out from a weekly national newspaper that we have subscribed to for many years. It is the *Spotlight*, a populist (shades of Jefferson) newspaper and prints all the news that the *New York Times* considers not fit to print. We get the truth about a lot of major news that other papers censor. They asked in one spot for suggestions of projects that we thought important to cover.

I suggested a section on religion analysis, and a complete coverage of the alien plane crash fifty years ago in Roswell, New Mexico. Rather than recite briefly here what I sent them, I am enclosing a copy of my letter to them. I sent them copies of my pamphlets plus Jennie's "Biblical Women." I just sent them two days ago, so no answer yet. I have high hopes, but am ready for disappointment,

I have also included two documents on some of my military service. I gather that your father was in the military, and you might be interested to see that I have sometimes been busy during my life. No glory or greatness, but I have tried to do the jobs that God gives me to do, as well as I can, with the limited abilities with which He has blessed me . . . .

With all of our love, Jennie and Don

July 10, 1997

Mr. Vince Ryan, Senior Editor, The Spotlight

300 Independence Avenue, SE, Washington, DC 20003

Dear Vince:

I have enclosed your survey, together with a few documents in connection with my recommendations for your consideration.

Our so-called "Christian" religion in this world is founded so very much on sand and fairy tales instead of on truth that it is due for extinction in some near century. Perhaps some day it will be founded on the real live Jesus who performed such a wonderful missionary project throughout the Roman Empire for thirty-five years after he came down from the cross. He gets no credit at all for that performance. His son and grandson get no credit for following in his footsteps after his retirement in A.D. 70. The entire record is in the Dead Sea Scrolls, plus the Book of Revelation.

The history of Jesus and his works is recorded in the book *Jesus and the Riddle of the Dead Sea Scrolls*, also published as *Jesus the Man*, plus the book *Jesus of the Apocalypse,* both written by Dr. Barbara Thiering, and published by Doubleday. She was connected with the University of Sydney School of Theology. She has her degree of Ph.D. in theology. She and Geza Vermes are the two greatest experts in the world in Greek and Hebrew in connection with Dead Sea Scrolls. She read and studied the scrolls for twenty years from 1967 to 1987, taking notes, calculating chronology, and the like. Vermes is just as good, but he is a French Catholic priest, and the pope will not let him publish any history from the scrolls recorded after 100 B.C.

In connection with my recommendation on the Roswell crash of an alien plane, General Arthur Trudeau, head of Army Research and Development, with the terrific aid of Colonel Philip Corso, had charge of the incredulous treasure trove of military and civilian materials and devices, re-trieved from the wreck, and four dead bodies, which were sent to Walter Reed and Bethesda Hospitals for complete autopsies.

They respected the cover-up imposed by the military to prevent panic, but went to work devising and implementing a plan to funnel all of the gigantic information obtained from the crash into public channels. They planned to avoid panic while creating the maximum benefits to the military and the entire country.

Crash items were passed to various defense contractors to be developed in their own research departments. Fiber-optics circuits without poles or wires went to the Bell Labs. Accelerated particle beam went to General Electric. Incidentally, from that beam we got our microwave oven. High tenacity fabric gave us the Kevlar bulletproof vest.

Other benefits included the laser cutting tool and SDI Strategic Defense Initiative or Star Wars. That beam locks into incoming warheads or vehicles electronically, penetrating them and exploding. It was devastating to the Iraqi tanks.

Permitting the various defense contractors to apply and receive patents in their own names, leaving out all reference to Roswell did all of this. This is all described in Colonel Corso's book, *The Day After Roswell,* published by Pocket Books. He was free to publish it under the new Freedom of Information Act; I have enclosed a copy of Senator Strom Thurmond's foreword in his book, If you have any means of contacting Senator Thurmond, he can fill you in real well. His book would be a wonderful addition to your Liberty Lobby Library.

I have covered only a few high spots here. It would be wonderful for a paper like yours, to which we have subscribed for many years, to give the public tremendous exposure to the work of two of the greatest American patriots of this century—General Arthur Trudeau and Colonel Philip Corso. Also add General Nathan Twining to them. He was in on the project in a big way.

I hope that I have given you some ideas for your great paper, even if you fear using some of them.

Cordially,

Commander Donald O. Burling, USNR (Ret) USNA, 1925 P. S. I served in World War II for five years, all of it at sea. I was executive officer on two large vessels, and ended up as commanding officer of another vessel.

December 14, 1997

Dear Dodie:

Jennie died December 3rd and was buried December 5th. It was sudden, although we all knew it was terminal, I thought she had a month or two more. She died at home, under Hospice care. They are a volunteer organization that serves the terminally ill, under a physician's recommendation. They are just great. She was on a hospital bed in the dining room. I slept in a guest bedroom next to her. Three Hospice people, a very close neighbor and his wife, and I were with her to the end. She died bravely and unafraid to the end, just as she had lived.

I must carry on as she would have me do and as I would do anyway. Over fifty people were at her viewing and at her graveside service. The minister was kind enough to recite her creed, and my creed, from Mark 12: 28:34. I am enclosing a copy of that service.

I'm sorry I did not call, but I was awfully busy. Darrel is the only one that I called at the time. Two years ago since her treatment she fought the battle but now has lost. I am enclosing our Christmas card to all on both her Christmas list and mine, with a note that goes with all of them. She was a strong, brave woman, Dodie, and I was lucky to have her for fifty years.

We both love you, Dodie, and I will still stay close to you as long as I am here. I will carry on the best that I can. Jennie never quit, and neither will I. With loads of love, Don

May 8, 1998

Dear Dodie:

Here it is finally. I have stalled on composing this data for a long time, simply because I was afraid that I could not do it right. But your last letter sort of told me that I had to try to do it. So I sat down and started it, and kept at it for two weeks. Surprisingly to me, the words poured out very easily. This is the best that I can do. I have hit the high spots, and hope that this gives you a framework that you can use to work in anything else that you please. It may suggest a lot of questions that you may want to ask. Write them down, and I will answer them the best that I can. I have run off only thirty copies. They will be used only for especially close friends. You may use the data any way that you please. My only target is that my life experiences may inspire some others to improve their own life experiences.

With very much love, Don

P.S. Today is my Golden Wedding Anniversary.

May 28, 1998

Dear Dodie:

Enclosed is a wonderful surprise that I never counted on.
Two months ago I took Jennie's notes and a letter (most of
which is printed herewith) down to our local weekly newspaper. I offered them as a contribution for their Memorial
Day issue. They put them on the front page, with Jennie's
picture in uniform. The notes will contain serially for three
or four weeks till completed. I won't send the additional
issues, as you have her complete notes already. It was a
wonderful Golden Wedding Anniversary present for both
Jennie and me.

Your flower arrangement arrived OK, and was beautiful.
Thank you for your thoughtfulness.

I hope my little thesis gives you a good framework for a
better job. My only hope is that it will inspire some others to
improve their own plans, with greater appreciation and
service for God.

With great love, Don

July 20, 1998

Dear Dodie

Your wonderful letter came at a very good time. It was a great day-brightener for me. I have been getting a bit discouraged, especially with my hearing worsening badly since Jennie died. . . .

I have enclosed a set of anecdotes for you to consider fitting into our book. I think that they would spice it up a little bit. I have also included a small list of people who could clue you in to more information about Jennie and me.

I have also included the newspaper record of my graduation. Maybe you can scan it into a fairly legible picture. I am the third midshipman from President Coolidge in the picture. The fifth in line was my roommate, John Burton. We got our diplomas in alphabetical order. The paper photographer took the picture at just the right time.

I hope that you can read my handwriting. I have arthritis in two fingers, and can use the typewriter with only my two index fingers. I can type one or two pages quite good, but not a large number of pages. . . .

I sure hope that Oprah will pick us up and help us. It would sure be a crowning glory for an old man to leave this life with a final victory. But one thing you can be sure of, Dodie, I never quit, and I never will, win or lose.

With greatest love, for an unusual great friendship for two fighters that have helped each other so much.

I love you, Don Burling

December 10, 1998

Dear Dodie,

I do hope that our book is still alive. I realize that this is the final big stage to get it ready for a publisher. I hope that we have enough material for a respectable size book. I am working on two final anecdotes. I have all of the material for them. It is just a matter of determining the best wording. Together they will not exceed eight typewritten pages. We have lost Jennie's body, but maybe we can give her a monument that will preserve her great courage and dedication for a long time. I would never be the man that I am today except for her fifty years of high level dedication, love and support. And she lived that same courage for many years before she even met me. . . .

I am always with you, Don

December 21, 1998

Dear Dodie,

I never thought much about adding some of my poetry to our book, but lately I have thought that it would serve a useful purpose as an addendum to our book. I have written poetry even since I was twelve years old. In my more mature years I have tried to blend together a useful mixture of philosophy, religion and accurate history, in a setting of teaching a lesson. I have always been an educator, but never a missionary.

Most of my work has been lost. Seventy-five years of many changes of location, five years of war, two wives, and radical changes in lifestyle, have lost most of my records and possessions. The enclosed poems are some of my best that I have succeeded in preserving. As an addendum they will stand on their own, without competing with the main frame of our book.

I rely on you to use them as you see fit. In my earlier life, I was a great fan of Shakespeare. I admired his clever use of long poetry, with perfect meter, to arrange his stories. I have copied his meter arrangement in the first poem. . .

I hope that our book is still in the mainstream of preparation. It would be so wonderful to build this monument for Jennie, and keep her terrific inspiration, dedication and unselfishness alive for many other people, even though her body is gone. She lived her whole life this way, since long before I even met her. I think that it is accurate to say that she doubled my inspiration and dedication during our fifty years of partnership.

I still live in hope that we will succeed. My love and prayers are with you, Dodie, especially in my regular prayer that I offer up to God twice a day. That prayer is as long as most ministers sermons, but that communication time belongs to God, and He gets it, twice a day.

With the greatest love, Don

January 6, 1999

Dear Dodie

I have not been able to construct any more anecdotes in satisfactory shape. But suddenly a lightning bolt hit my brain, and the message was "send Dodie some of your poems." So that is what I did. I hope you can use some of them, but censor where you think it is best.

Enclosed are five sheets. The first is a correction on page eighteen of my booklet. It took me some time of additional proofreading to note that the last two lines of verse XXV of the long poem were missing. I copied a sheet with the error instead of a corrected sheet. Will you exchange it for the sheet you presently have?

The hymn is my favorite of all the hymns that I have written. I wrote it after our album was published. It can be sung to the tune of "Whispering Hope" or to Yanok's tune. I think Yanok did a very good job with it. Will you judge whether it is better to include it with the album tunes or separately with the other poems in the booklet, or just omit it? I trust your judgement.

My life has been built since my teenage period on a foundation of religion, philosophy, psychology and historical accuracy. I always try to sprinkle in a fair ration of comedy and fantasy, wherever it seems appropriate. I hope that these parables and some true stories of history give you some pleasure.

The poems on the so-called Battle of Lexington were written as part of my thesis in a course on Research in connection with my work for my master's degree in Education. Our professor was Dr. Fiori, an accomplished historian. The research on the tiny incident at Lexington constituted the entire course on Research. The thesis substituted for final examination on the course. I got an A in it. The professor gave us a generous amount of resources to search out for the true information. It sure opened my eyes to see how most historians have bungled that battle. Actually, the British Company had only one objective, and that was to destroy the rebel's giant military supplies at Concord. They had strict orders not to let any other activity interfere with that objective.

Much of the poems that I have written have been lost, due to very frequent changes in location and activities over a seventy-year period. The war interfered greatly in keeping records. They were left with my first wife during my five years of continuous sea duty. Since I did not go back with her after the war, they were lost. Incidentally, Darrel found my Annapolis diploma among Flora's effects when she died in 1984, and sent it to me.

We have lost Jennie's body, but maybe we can make her deep inspiration, courage and dedication live for a long time to help a great many other people. It would be a wonderful monument for such a great courageous woman. The book would be a most wonderful way for me to end this life.

All my love to you Dodie. We have never seen each other, but our friendship far exceeds that of most people who have been together physically for a long time. I hope we succeed.

Love and prayers, hope and thanks for your work, Don

Index

B

USS *Ulysses S. Grant*, 11
USS *Vega*, 30, 31, 41, 42, 67
USS *West Point*, 28, 30, 33, 41, 42, 57
V
Vermes, Geza, 152, 157
W
Wagers, Ralph, 16
Wakefield, 29
Walter Reed Hospital, 69, 157
Washington, D.C., 12
Washington, George, 24, 45
Washington, North Carolina, 21
Waterville, Maine, 22, 64
Weymouth, Massachusetts, 34
White Gumbo, 16, 17, 18
Wilbur, Secretary, 43
Williams, Hank, 10
Wilson, Barbara, 14
Wilson, Beverly, 14
Wilson, Frederick M., 14
Wilson, Jessie Davis, 14
Wilson, Richard, 14
Wilson, Rosamond, 14
World War I, 14, 63, 143
World War II, ix, 8
World War II Victory Medal, 11
Y
Yanok, Tom, 141, 144, 165
Yokohama, 11
Z
Zola, Emile, 63, 65